CHANGE YOUR MINDSET, *NOT YOUR MAN*

Learn to Love **What's Right** Instead of Trying to Fix **What's Wrong**

Sally B. Watkins, MSW

adam

Avon, Mass

D0062553

Copyright © 2009 by Sally B. Watkins
All rights reserved.
This book, or parts thereof, may not be reproduced in any
form without permission from the publisher; exceptions are
made for brief excerpts used in published reviews.

Published by
Adams Media, a division of F+W Media, Inc.
57 Littlefield Street, Avon, MA 02322. U.S.A.
www.adamsmedia.com

ISBN 10: 1-60550-142-5
ISBN 13: 978-1-60550-142-0

Printed in the United States of America.

J I H G F E D C B A

Library of Congress Cataloging-in-Publication Data
is available from the publisher.

This publication is designed to provide accurate and authoritative information
with regard to the subject matter covered. It is sold with the understanding that
the publisher is not engaged in rendering legal, accounting, or other professional
advice. If legal advice or other expert assistance is required, the services of a
competent professional person should be sought.

  —From a *Declaration of Principles* jointly adopted by a Committee of the
American Bar Association and a Committee of Publishers and Associations

Many of the designations used by manufacturers and sellers to distinguish their
product are claimed as trademarks. Where those designations appear in this
book and Adams Media was aware of a trademark claim, the designations have
been printed with initial capital letters.

This book is available at quantity discounts for bulk purchases.
For information, please call 1-800-289-0963.

CONTENTS

INTRODUCTION

Many women feel that the way to fix a problem is to confront their man, reveal their feelings, and ask for what they want to change. If you've tried this typical tactic, you may have already discovered that in most cases one of two things happened: (1) complaining or criticizing him only made the problem worse, or (2) things improved for a little while and then went back to the way they were before. In this book I will share what I've learned from a lifetime of my own relationships, and from the hundreds of clients who have trusted me to guide them to a happier, more fulfilling place. Unlike other self-help books or couples' counseling, my approach offers some breakthrough beliefs and processes.

Relationships Start Backward

Perhaps because of humans' strong biological need to maintain the species, we are at the peak of our relationship fervor when we first meet and feel attracted to each other. After a while, however, the best behavior that you wore in the early stages of courtship relaxes into something more natural, and the powerful brain chemistry that provided a sense of euphoria, heightened attachment, and excitement dissipates. You may be in the early stages of your commitment, having moved in together or married, when the hard work of the relationship begins. The powerful projections put forth by both partners—that this person is perfect, the ideal, a soul mate—disappear and you may believe that they have changed.

For example, my client Laurie remembers the terrible pain she felt when it seemed all too apparent that her whirlwind romance with Quinn had settled into a familiar pattern after two years of marriage. "He sits through dinner preoccupied with work and talks about all the technical problems he is having with some device there. He drinks the rest of the bottle of wine after I consume just a few ounces. He has nothing personal to say to me. I'm not interested in sex when he comes to bed after watching TV all night. I feel like I've been installed as *the wife* and he can go back to his real priorities. It's devastating." Laurie cries as she tells me these painful revelations and, like most in long-term relationships, there have been countless tears. This is the point in the process where it seems as if everything has changed—and in fact it has changed.

You Are in Good Company

Romantic movies, romance novels, TV sitcoms, love-oriented music lyrics, and reports of famous people coupling and uncoupling all reflect society's preoccupation with finding a perfect mate and creating a powerful and lasting love bond. Those who are frustrated believe they are in the minority, when in fact they are more often the norm. You may be saying, *Wait a minute, isn't it right to expect that a partner will meet my needs in the relationship? Isn't that what we were promised?* The short answer is no. Life hands us a certain number of pains, upsets, problems, and pitfalls. A relationship is a risk: an adventure with no guarantees.

Some women have given up trying to make things better and live in continual grief and despair of what might have been. Most try to improve their situation by arguing and confronting, crying and complaining, hoping and waiting, or eventually by separating, divorcing, or by having affairs and looking outside their relationship for what's missing. Some go to counseling only to find out that the solution to their conflict isn't easily available, or that the process of bringing all the problems and bad feelings into the open actually makes the hurt, anger, and ultimately the relationship worse. Does this sound like you? This book is for you if:

- You are disappointed with your current relationship.
- You ended previous relationships because he didn't measure up to what you wanted.
- You have failed to fix your relationship by explaining to him what you need and want to be happy.
- You have tried self-help books and couples' counseling but they didn't correct the problem.
- He seems to improve for a while after you complain to him, but eventually goes back to his old ways.
- You argue with him about his behavior and both of you end up feeling angry, upset, and distant.
- You feel hopeless about changing him to be the way you want—the way you believe he was when you first met.
- You are sick and tired of always feeling angry, negative, hurt, upset, and irritated about your relationship.
- You view other women as happier in their relationship and more successful in creating a relationship than you have been.
- You believe that he has the ability to be a better partner but is too lazy or indifferent, or has other priorities.

- It feels as though you are the only one trying to improve the relationship.
- Most of your relationships end up the same way, with the same types of problems or issues, even though they seem different at first.
- Your partner doesn't see the same problems in the relationship that you do.
- You wonder if your relationship is salvageable or if it's just too far gone.

Consider a Relationship's Purpose

I want to propose something radical: That the purpose of a relationship is not to make you happy—no one person can or should be expected to do that—but rather to help you evolve and grow in character and strength and support your being in the world. A relationship shows you your own issues, your own psychological work, and what you need to become for your own maturity. A good relationship is not *out there* for you to find in the form of a perfect mate, but inside of you in the form of a stronger, more resilient self. If you leave a relationship without coming to terms with your issues there is a high likelihood that you will attract and form another very similar relationship in the future.

This book will show you that there are ways to be fully present without transforming your partner but by changing the way you see him. Becoming more conscious, mindful, and observant of both yourself and your thoughts will give you more behavioral options. As you become healthier, more mature, and better able to take responsibility for your needs and nurture yourself, you'll discover that you're not a victim in the relationship, but an active co-creator. You'll learn to ask for what you want without being attached to the outcome, and will experience a decrease in anger and disappointment as you depend more on your own resources.

There may be some grief and loss as you accept that the idealized fantasy of the perfect pair is not something that can be attained, and that even your need for sensitive mirroring and cherishing by your mate may not be realistic. You may be willing to accept that looking repeatedly for the *right* person is energy misplaced and focus instead on changing the way you see yourself, your partner, and what you can create together. My hope is that this book will be the lens through which you'll be able to see the opportunities, the positives, and the strengths in your relationship, and—more important—help you get on with your life and create something that is ultimately full, rich, and satisfying.

Disclaimer

Please keep in mind that the concepts and suggestions presented here are for relationships in which abuse is not an issue. If physical, emotional, or verbal abuse is a problem in your relationship it is important that you seek professional help and do not attempt to apply the recommendations described in this book.

PART ONE

THE ENLIGHTENED MINDSET

You, as an individual woman, are the focus of Part I. Here you'll find the essential things you must know and understand to be enlightened about yourself, your life, and your relationships. Cultural myths and expectations of romantic love have contributed to your disappointment with relationships. Learning about your childhood and past partners will help you recognize where your current issues may have originated and teach you how to deal with them. Analyzing the connection between your thoughts and feelings provides an effective tool for managing moods and emotions. Stories are not always innocent and may affect your feelings of closeness; recognizing how and why you tell them may be a revelation to you. Experiencing your full range of emotions and accepting the necessary pain of life will ultimately provide you with the most satisfaction and happiness. Embracing these concepts may change the course of your life and your relationships.

CHAPTER 1

FAIRYTALE FANTASY—BUSTED!

As a culture, we support the delusion that the fairytale wedding is the beginning of happily-ever-after, and we have come to believe in this ideal as the gold standard of a relationship. Additionally, women are invested in their own entitlement: the idea that it's your right as a woman to have wonderful cherishing relationships and that anything less is settling or selling out. Even in the face of multiple relationship failures you may believe that the perfect person is out there and that you can either find him or restyle your current man to be him.

Where did the idea of this *perfect* relationship come from? Throughout history, you'll see economic and social needs taking precedence in a marriage partnership. In fact, it wasn't until the 1800s that marrying for love became common. Even today, in countries with arranged marriages, there is an unstated contract governing gender roles and expectations, and romantic love is neither expected nor required.

In this modern era, many traditional reasons for marriage have been eliminated: women can now acquire property, have careers, and support themselves and their children financially. Today, many women want to find and be with a soul mate who will complete them—a goal guaranteed to meet with obstacles.

Without a reasonably good relationship model to draw from while growing up, many women may have substituted a fantasy ideal instead. They rejected the problematic relationship of their parents and imagined something perfect for themselves.

Unveil the Delusion

The bitter potion that you may find hard to swallow is that, if you persist in your delusion about having a fairytale relationship, you may morph from the beautiful princess into a dark queen; you will be the one creating havoc in the kingdom when your anger and resentment boil over. In this real world of imperfect humans, you need to realize that your man can't fulfill this fantasy. I have seen my share of women—beginning with my mother—whose dreams of happily ever after were never realized; their pain is palpable. I also know firsthand how it feels when your hopes and expectations of a perfect relationship begin to diminish and nothing you do can convince your "Prince Charming" that he already has everything you need; he just needs to provide it.

 I'm fifty-five and have been married to a slug for twenty-five years. Why do I start fights to try to get him to care even a little?—*Tina*

DEAR TINA: You may have a connection with him that depends on feeling bad. See if you can harvest all the energy you are expending on anger and suffering and focus on creating some good in your life.

Right now stop everything—the nagging, coaching, and cajoling, and especially the pouting, crying, and acting out your misery. Cease complaining to your partner, but also to your mother, sisters, and girlfriends. Until you can find a different perspective, don't even run these negative scenarios through your head. You need clarity and this book will provide it, but for now begin by giving up the practices that are exacerbating your problems.

Don't Expand the Problem

Your intentions were good. You may have thought, *if I tell him what I need or what he's doing that hurts my feelings he'll change and our relationship will be back on track.* However, you may also already have an inkling that your words are falling on deaf ears. Perhaps, as you say these words to him, he escapes to the garage or picks up the TV remote. Maybe it's even worse than that. As you escalate your attempts to get through to him, he may be building an impenetrable fortress to defend himself from you, and may not remember anything that you're saying. I've seen men who haven't had a clue what their women have been saying to them, and only remember that they've been complaining—a lot!

Stop Complaining

Please let me be your Fairy Godmother today and tell you that complaining is not the solution to your problem. Even if your man tries to listen and does some things to please you, it will be short-lived and he'll eventually revert back to his familiar patterns. There is a way to change this picture and I'll explain it to you—but for now, dry your eyes, go to the mirror-mirror on the wall, and give yourself a pep talk that goes like this: There is no one to blame here, especially not _____. I've tried to get him to be more attentive and affectionate, but I'm releasing myself from the task of changing him and releasing him from my need for him to change. Instead, I'm going to focus on changing the only one I can change—me.

This is a huge leap and one that may take awhile to completely accept and practice. To help you there are several ways that you can reinforce this new idea. Write in the margins of your day planner, make a sticky note for your computer or dashboard, or with a fine indelible marker and a ribbon make a bracelet for your wrist with this message: *Let him be as he is*. Some of my clients use just the initials l-h-b-a-h-i to keep their mantra private. You need this constant reminder to truly practice this solution. It is critical to your success and is the most difficult to undertake.

Surrender Your Cherished Belief

I will warn you that it may feel like your heart is breaking when you give up this cherished belief. I certainly felt that way! Being loved by a good man was the thing I wanted above all else. As I began to accept that the man I idealized did not exist and that the relationship I craved would never happen, I felt heartsick. I recalled everything that I did and sacrificed while looking for love and felt ashamed and humiliated. But I also felt compassion for that naïve, needy girl who invested so much in the fairytale that she now realized was an illusion.

Men and Women *Are* Different

One of life's realities that you need to consider is that men and women are not only hormonally different, but are also socialized to want vastly different things.

The Female Experience

The female's nature and conditioning conspire to emphasize feminine virtues like sensitivity and caring for others, making relationships and attracting a man a high priority. While getting an education and finding a job are often practical necessities, it is woman's biological destiny to bear and raise children, make a nest, and integrate caregiving into whatever else is also important to her.

 How can I stop comparing my husband with my friends' husbands who seem way more attentive than mine?—*Rachel*

DEAR RACHEL: You harbor a delusion that there is a perfect man, and in order to support your fantasy you selectively look at traits. This is dangerous since the greener grass over the fence still has the same crabgrass. Look at the bigger picture of your relationship for a more balanced view.

The Male Experience

Your man, however, is biologically and culturally conditioned to suppress his feelings, develop courage, and compete with other men as a precursor to becoming the family protector and making his mark in the world. In fact, the latest research shows that males actually have smaller centers in their brain for communication and emotional processing. The typical man is one who doesn't have relationships as a top priority or goal, admits to being mystified by women, and has little understanding of women's moods and feelings. In fact, your man may even believe that—like the fairytale prince—all that is expected of him is to prove his worthiness for the princess' hand in marriage. He thinks those difficult challenges are behind him at the wedding, while you may see it as only the beginning of the *happily ever after* he is going to provide.

Men and Women Have Different Visions

While most women's vision is centered on the home and family, men are trained to focus on the wider world and often spend considerable energy mastering something that others deem important. His team winning the championship or him identifying with an action adventure hero can be a substitute for this. It's a rude awakening for a man to learn that his woman is unhappy and he may not understand how he could be the cause. It's likely that he will tune her out if he is unable to feel successful with her and turn his attention to another activity where he can achieve positive feedback.

So, when a woman comes to my office to regale me with stories of her man's ineptitude, indifference, lack of warmth and affection, and inability to relate to her as she desperately wants, she needs to understand that it's not totally his fault. His role as a partner is no doubt important to him, but his bigger interest lies in doing something great in the world or expressing his manhood in a symbolic way outside the relationship, and that's not a bad thing. For example, even if you both have difficult, demanding jobs, they will probably mean different things to each of you. His will probably be tied up with his ego, his manhood, getting recognition, and supporting his family. Yours may be about raising your living standard, saving for your kids' education, or fulfilling a desire to serve. Even if your money is an economic necessity, you and your man are probably oriented differently to the work you do. There are those who will deny these observations and profess a more gender-neutral world, but I believe the contrary.

Women Invest More in a Relationship

Who you are as a woman is not primarily riding on your work performance or income as it usually is for a man. As a woman, your good feelings about yourself may have more to do with how successfully you have attracted a man and how much he adores and cherishes you. Women often compete in this regard. Typically women clients will tell me that they see their friends, relatives, and coworkers with enviable spouses and perfect marriages and think to themselves *what's wrong with me?* The truth is that nothing is wrong with you. The glasses you're looking through are distorting your vision. You can't know from the outside what a couple's relationship is really like. It's unlikely that most women are receiving all the devotion and love that they might want from their man.

Don't Buy Into the Relationship Myth

It's not your fault that you developed this belief system. The movies you may have grown up with—especially Disney movies like *The Little Mermaid* or *Sleeping Beauty* to name a few—have not demonstrated a healthy relationship dynamic and instead supported the fantasy of an ideal relationship. Every one of these films focuses on the sexual attraction between the young hero and heroine and their ultimate happiness together. The fantasy says that relationships shouldn't take any work and will arrive fully formed when the hero and heroine fatefully connect. You can see everywhere in movies, romance novels, tabloids, and sitcoms how American culture glorifies sexual and romantic love and perpetrates this myth.

Unfortunately, when you believe this myth and function this way in your relationship, you limit yourself to a childlike frame of mind—you stay immature and dependent, hoping and waiting like Cinderella for a prince to improve your life and fulfill your dreams. Instead, you should strive to create a brand new version of your relationship in which the challenges and learning opportunities enable you to grow in maturity.

TRY THIS   Discover Your Relationship View

1   How do I see myself in relation to my man—as an equal but different partner or as dependent on a certain kind of love from him to complete me?

2   How do my need for signs of love and attention and my attempts to get them affect the relationship?

3   Am I growing as a more evolved person in this relationship or swirling in negative emotions?

4   Am I building a case for my belief (for example, that my partner doesn't love or care for me or that he isn't the right one for me), or can I consider a more balanced view?

Get Out of the Victim Trap

You are probably aware of how women are victimized by the media and portrayed as sexual objects with body images that are totally unattainable for the average woman. The relationship victim trap, however, is less well known but more insidious—it keeps women immature and dependent on men for their primary fulfillment. By breaking through this erroneous definition of relationship you will be taking a big step for yourself and another big step for womankind.

I will show you that, by growing up and becoming a fully mature woman, your relationship can bloom into something that will work in a real life way and be satisfying on many levels. Accepting responsibility for your part of the dilemma can reenergize your relationship and allow you to take a step toward conscious womanhood, a place of true beauty and radiance.

Respect Comes Before Love

You may recognize that if your man made you and your feelings the center of his existence and gave up what was important to him in order to please you, you'd probably disrespect him, maybe even despise him. To keep your trust, respect, and love, he has to show strength of character and autonomy, and demonstrate the integrity that makes you admire him. He must have a greater purpose than your relationship and be successful in worldly pursuits or you'll see him as weak because he was so easily manipulated in succumbing to your desires. You should be relieved that your man didn't yield to your demand that he change. He will be more sexy and attractive to you if he can maintain his strong, authentic persona. You may not see this now, but in time you will recognize his resistance as a blessing.

Acceptance Is Power

I want you to find your true self, your biggest best feminine evolution, your wild and wonderful soulful existence, your fullness, your ecstatic love of life that only a totally grounded woman could have. And then I want you to be with your partner as he is without trying to change him. My challenge to you is to grow, inspire each other, learn how to be in a real relationship with your partner, and, more important, learn how to be with yourself. This won't be an easy ride in a pumpkin carriage. Instead it will demand everything of you.

 I am having a hard time with the acceptance idea. Isn't that just giving up on him when I know he's capable of more?—*Lorraine*

DEAR LORRAINE: Your non-acceptance hasn't been working for you, has it? Try acknowledging the positives and see what changes for you or for him. You may get the more you are wanting.

Surrender the Child Version of Relationship

Karen, now forty-eight years old, had two marriages and a long-term, live-in boyfriend before she met and married Greg, a childless widower. He is a physician and she is a nurse educator in the hospital where they met. Karen so longed for a love connection that she plunged into marriage with Greg and feared that this was yet another relationship that wasn't going to make it. "I had qualms about marrying him," She told me at our first session. "But my kids liked him, and my friends thought he was a great catch. But even while we were on our honeymoon he was doing stock trades, keeping track of patient problems, working out, and playing golf. I felt like a tag-along."

Recently, Karen started on an antidepressant to deal with her negativity, insomnia, and irritability. As an only child of parents who owned their own small auto repair business and worked long hours, she buried herself in books and school. Cared for by a devoted grandmother, she saw her weary parents for only a few hours each night and never felt important or cherished by them. Not surprisingly, Karen was attracted to men who had demanding careers and had difficulty paying attention to her as well. Food became a replacement for the missing love and Karen complains she's even less attractive to Greg since gaining weight.

Despite her incredible intellect and successful career, Karen still holds a childlike view of a relationship and dreams of a powerful man sweeping her up on his steed and galloping them off to a life of devotion and love. She's magnified what's missing from her life, and every sign that Greg's preoccupation is not with her and their relationship stabs at her heart. She reluctantly admits that there are a lot of positive things about her life now. Greg is committed to educating her two children and considers them his own. He gives them a high standard of living and wonderful family vacations. He gifts her with beautiful jewelry, which she rarely wears. They have an active social life based around the symphony where he is a major contributor. However, Karen laments, "It's mostly his money he gives me. I want more of *him*."

Karen agreed to look at the bigger picture and what she discovered surprised her. Practicing the affirmation *I am open to receive love in all its forms and in all ways* was, at first, a teeth-gritting mantra as she struggled to drop the negativity that she had held onto for so long. But, by reframing events to see the positive, she began to soften and experience love in its broadest definition. When she dropped her preoccupation with Greg, the world became brighter, the roses in her yard smelled sweeter, and the interest of her friends felt warmer. When they went to a symphony fundraiser where Greg was an officer, Karen stood back from the crowd and, instead of feeling ignored and devalued, saw how his commitment to giving and supporting the arts blessed her and gave her more stature in the community. Afterward she reported that, instead of overeating, complaining about her boring evening, and making him wrong for his behavior, she complimented him and said something like, *I'm proud to be with you when you take on this work for the community.*

Karen said that they actually made love that night. "He commented on how beautiful I looked. I think the difference in my appearance was that I was more open, more positive." In the following weeks Karen saw that, while Greg cared a lot about money and the things that it would buy, he had a generosity of spirit that she could view as a loving gesture. Especially when it came to her two children, she felt grateful.

Gratitude Expands Your View

Gratitude is closely connected to happiness. People who note the things that make them grateful—from everyday things like the air they breathe to beautiful sunsets to acts of kindness from others or events that turn out well—report more positive feelings and less depression. Karen began wearing the beautiful jewelry that Greg had bought her over the years. He enjoyed seeing it on her even with t-shirts and jeans, and she used it as a reminder of the intangible ways he loved her.

Entitlement Is Off-Putting

Entitlement—a state demonstrated by Cinderella's spoiled stepsisters—is the sense that you are owed something. Do you feel angry or hurt if you did not receive the respect or attention you

Love Is Abundant

1   Throughout the day practice this affirmation: *I am open to receive love in all its forms and in all ways.* Test out this affirmation with everything that happens, even those things that at first appear unwanted or negative. See if it fits in some way. The idea is to expand your definition of love from a narrow fantasy to accepting love in other manifestations and from other things and people—a smile, a beautiful flower, a parking place, a helpful clerk.

2   Consider sending love and healing to those situations and people who irritate and exasperate you regularly. Recognize that responding in kind to bad behavior doesn't make you feel good and rarely improves the outcome.

felt you were entitled to? If so, it is better to use this realization to humble those entitled feelings than to strengthen them by complaining to others. Interpreting what your partner says or does as a personal attack or claiming that he makes you feel insecure may cause him to see you as difficult. Give up that line entirely—you know, the one that begins *you make me feel.* By attributing your feelings to his behavior you will be expending your energy focusing on him rather than seeing where you may need to change. Walking on eggshells and tiptoeing around a high-maintenance woman can be stressful for your partner.

When you act like the princess in "The Princess and the Pea" who can still feel a pea under eighteen mattresses, your partner may decide you can't ever be pleased and will stop trying. I can hear you asking, *You mean if someone hurts my feelings I shouldn't tell them about it?* The short answer is no. This advice, of course, assumes that there was no intention of hurting your feelings in the first place. It is an impossible task to try to teach people to be the way you want them to be. You will only be creating distance and conflict by expecting them to know and provide the sensitivity you need. When you feel hurt or angry it is an opportunity for you to support yourself and accept that others are imperfect and can't always be as caring as you would like.

Look Within

When your feelings are hurt, take the opportunity to consider whether this is an old wound from the past surfacing in another form or if you are sensitive for another reason. It would be better for you to allow these hurt feelings to work themselves out rather than trying to shape your world and your mate into being different so you don't have to experience them. It is ultimately more rewarding to allow people to be as they are.

When she understood herself and her childhood better, Karen realized that she couldn't expect that Greg would make up for what she didn't get growing up with busy, distracted parents. It became apparent to her that she would have to find the support and love to be alright within herself—even without constant reassurance in the form of affection and attention from him. She was surprised that when she was not appreciated she could actually tolerate some intense pain, accept that it was old stuff, and let it be OK. Over time, these feelings lessened and became more manageable.

Giving up the antidepressants was the next step in her process and she learned to deal with her emotions without them. She accepted that Greg worked hard to be highly regarded in the world. Karen also restructured her beliefs about Greg and understood that his lack of interest in her at times was not because he didn't love her.

Consider YOUR Mindset When women stop complaining, blaming, and explaining and realize that it is okay for their partner to be as he is, wonderful things may occur. You can also extend that same acceptance to yourself and let your feelings exist as they are without judging or trying to change them. Relationships help women mature and evolve through their adult lives. By breaking away from your preoccupation with how things ought to be—how love should be conveyed based on your fantasies and unrealistic stories of romantic love—you are taking a step toward a more realistic partnership based on self-responsibility.

Share YOUR Views At the end of every chapter I will propose some questions that would be useful to discuss with other women you know. A women's club, support group, church group, or your own circle of friends may be a place to share ideas about the topics explored in the chapter. This could be an informal occasional get-together or regularly scheduled meeting times for each of the fourteen chapters. The format is simply to let each woman answer a question and share her experience. Because each of you will have your own personal views and unique opinions the discussion can be an opportunity to learn from each other and come to a deeper understanding of these issues for yourself.

1 Has your dream life gotten in the way of your real life? Just as the media's beauty standards have made it hard to accept our normal bodies, has the myth of *happily ever after* contributed to disappointment with your relationship?

2 How do you take to the idea of allowing your partner to be as he is without pressuring him to be more attentive? What do you see happening for good or bad if you stopped trying to change him?

3 What experience have you had with gratitude? Has it made a difference in your mood or behavior?

CHAPTER 2

LOVE HISTORIES— THE NAKED REVEAL

Our relationship with our parents sets the stage for most of the relationships that follow. Some adults struggle to overcome their childhood wounding and continue to suffer the same issues with their current partners that they experienced as children. The most common emotional childhood wound is not being valued for your essential self, but instead for what you could supply for your caretakers. Many children, due to their need for love and approval, abandon this "unwanted" self and redesign themselves to be more pleasing to their parents. Today, the most difficult challenge for many people is to recognize and support their true, essential self and refuse to hide or deny themselves to earn love or to be what others want.

Those who were not blessed with good parenting may make many mistakes as they learn how to be in a relationship. As you go through this process, it's important to not make yourself wrong for what you didn't know then, but to recognize your struggles as steps toward health. Courage is required to feel your pain and not repress, deny, or medicate it with addictions. The reward for you will be more maturity, the ability to make real connections, and greater internal peace.

Life Gives Us Lessons

If you are lamenting your past and the mistakes you've made, remember that everything that happened to you growing up and in your past relationships was in service to the person you are becoming. Your past wasn't designed to hurt, victimize, shame, or humiliate you, although in some cases it may have. Rather, its purpose was to teach, strengthen, and show you the places where you needed to grow. Your task now is to learn those hard lessons and graduate to wisdom-hood, which is my word for the rewards that come from conscious living. Come out from behind the denial and regret and face up to what happened. After all, you suffered the pain, confusion, and anxiety and should now reap the benefits of all that anguish. It's like taking the most challenging classes and doing all the homework, but not getting the concepts, flunking the finals, and having to start all over again. This time around, you can get it right. Your life is depending on it.

Learning to Relate

Do you remember being loved, cherished, and well cared for, or did your parents lack parenting skills? Were you a delight or a burden for your parents? Were you loved for yourself or for what you could provide? These are important questions because your internalized sense of yourself is formed by these early attachments and continues to grow with feedback from others as you develop. Most people bury their feelings of not being loved or adequately cared for if that was the case. They develop a defense system to patch themselves together and go on with life, which is a useful compensation for doubts about worth, lovability, and belonging. Without this shell many would not be able to cope with the difficulties of adolescence and adulthood. As a woman, however, it's your nature to be open and undefended and it's important to work through the old issues that keep you closed and unreceptive. When a woman feels empowered and good about herself she is able to be who she is without artifice or pretense. She doesn't need to develop inauthentic personas as a way to please or manipulate others.

Twenty-eight-year-old Mattie's barriers started forming at the age of seven when her parents divorced. She lived with her depressed and moody mother, who brought multiple boyfriends into and out of Mattie's life. Mattie says, "My dad was my rock for the first few years after the divorce and I loved spending weekends with him. He took me on errands to the hardware store and car wash. We cooked kid food like spaghetti and pizza together."

But, at age twelve, Mattie's world crashed when her dad remarried and had two boys in close succession. She was now someone to babysit and be the housemaid. Everything was about *their* two boys and *their* new family. Mattie's adolescence was stormy; her dad criticized her choices in boyfriends, her giving up sports, and her failing grades. She believed she was no longer important to him and saw herself as the cause for his bad treatment. She also felt as though she wasn't good enough, that she couldn't be what he wanted; kids almost always blame themselves when things go wrong with their parents. Eventually, Mattie stopped seeing him and her two half brothers and is still angry sixteen years later.

When Mattie explored her relationship history she noticed that a pattern emerged as she began dating. In the beginning she could intuit and become whatever her partner wanted. Sound familiar? In her desire to attract a guy she was the perfect match—sexy and fun, always doing what he wanted. When she met Aaron who was struggling to build his motorcycle business, she wanted to show him how valuable she could be. She even tried to make Aaron need her by cooking for him, giving him massages, and helping him with his business.

Ask Sally I am very controlling of my boyfriend because I still have a fear of abandonment leftover from childhood. How do I stop?—*Tamara*

> DEAR TAMARA: Learn to recognize the fear and tell your boyfriend that your threat is coming from old childhood issues. If it isn't about him he may be able to support you.

If you carry this type of inadequacy with you into your relationships and aren't convinced of your own essential value, you—like Mattie—may attempt to earn love by being useful and needed. You don't want to be rejected or abandoned again, so early on you make pleasing him and responding to his needs the key element in your relationship. You may even deliberately pick guys who need you, believing that this is the basis for a lasting relationship.

Recognize Undoing

As a therapist, I see the pattern of undoing—something we carry out unconsciously—in many women's histories. We seek out a person similar to one of our parents and attempt to change the outcome. In Mattie's case, she replicates the wounding she experienced in childhood by dating men like Aaron who subtly use her, then feels abandoned and rejected when the men are indifferent to her needs and expect her to continue giving to them. Mattie's unconscious desire was that Aaron, unlike her parents, would reciprocate by being involved and interested in her, and would love her for herself not for what she could do for him. This didn't happen. Instead, Mattie actually abandoned herself by leaving her needs, feelings, and desires out of the equation.

Isn't it funny how so many women want to be loved for who they are, but then pretend to be someone else? Then, if they do find love, they're loved for who they pretended to be rather than for who they are.

There Is No Substitute for Parental Love

To graduate to wisdom-hood you must accept the hard truth that there is no substitute for parental love; a romantic partner will never compensate for what you missed as a child. You are never going to get that delighted, devoted unconditional love that a parent has for her offspring. It's sad but true. However, if you can accept that there are certain experiences that you will always be without, you'll do a better job of taking responsibility for yourself. You may actually get more of what you need in life because you won't be looking for unconditional love where it doesn't exist and you won't feel there's something wrong with you because you aren't finding it.

Like Mattie you can connect the dots between your childhood relationship with your parents and the way you interact with your current man. Look at your relationship and notice if anything is similar to what you might have experienced with your parents.

Don't Take the Revolving Door

You might believe that the problem with your relationship is that you picked the wrong man, unconsciously creating a problematic relationship with him, and that the answer is to leave and start over with someone new and different. Many women have taken that route and it is usually a revolving door back into another difficult relationship. If you've had several relationships, you may already realize that if you stay the same there is a strong likelihood that you will pick similar men and create an identical

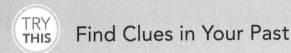

Find Clues in Your Past

Find a time and space where you can be alone, relax, and go back to your childhood. Look at your experience in three five-year blocks: birth to five years, five to ten years, and ten to fifteen years. Remember the details of where you lived, what your daily life was like, who was a part of your world at that time. See, hear, smell, taste, and feel how it was.

1   Describe your frustrations, your painful memories, and your problems.

2   Explain how you coped or reacted to these events.

3   What was the response from your parents?

4   What did you conclude about yourself as a result of these experiences?

5   How are your romantic relationships similar to or different from these early relationships?

6   What might you be trying to find in a partner to make up for what you didn't get growing up?

relationship dynamic over and over again. Each new relationship may look different at first, but will eventually settle into a familiar groove. Look at your childhood and relationship history for the places where you need to change—and where *you* need to become the person that you're looking for. A new partner is rarely the answer.

Don't Blame Your Parents

Maybe you grew up without the kind of loving attention that you needed. Perhaps your material needs were attended to but the circumstances you were born into did not provide as well for you emotional and psychological development. Coming to terms with your childhood isn't about blaming your parents. Maybe they couldn't parent you better because of their own upbringing, inadequacies, stressors, or situation. I often ask my clients: *Do you believe your parents could have given you the love, support, or care you needed and chose to deny you? Or do you believe that they did the best they could, that they didn't have it to give you, and that it just wasn't possible for them to do better?* Most of the time the answer is the latter.

There is a benefit in believing the second choice. Since you didn't live your parents' life and can't know the absolute truth, it's preferable to believe that they had your best interests at heart despite their behavior. This opens the door to letting old grievances, hurts, and anger dissolve and keeps you from feeling like a victim. It's time for you to move on past your childhood and begin taking responsibility for your own life.

Discover Clues from Your Parents

1   Make a list of the good qualities you saw in your parents.

2   Make a list of the qualities you did not like in your parents.

3   Make a list of the good qualities in your partner.

4   Make a list of the qualities you do not like in your partner.

5   Compare your lists and connect the attributes that are similar for both your parents and partner.

6   Circle those things in your parents that you currently see in yourself.

Let Go of Pain and Anger

It helps to bring those old wounds into the present day and do something about them, rather than stay focused on the past. Holding on to anger, pain, and negative emotions from the past can even hurt your body; it ties up energy and contributes to depression and physical ailments. Step up to your mirror right now, look yourself in the eye, and allow yourself to accept that the past is over. You didn't get all you would have wanted, but you can heal or rebuild yourself in the damaged or wounded places and it usually won't be necessary to break up with your partner to do that.

Notice when your regressed feelings surface and just allow them. If your partner unintentionally said or did something that hurt you or if you are experiencing emotions that seem too much for the situation, then your unresolved childhood issues may have been triggered. You can check this out by determining whether these feelings are similar to those you had growing up. What you don't give energy to will wane, so try tolerating the bad feelings and let them work themselves out without attempting to fix or change anything.

Learn from Relationship Failures

Don't be hard on yourself if your early attempts at finding a partner failed. Look at yourself and your relationship successes and failures in an objective way and learn from them. When we are critical and negative about our choices or our behavior it's human to push them into the junk closet of our memory bank. Today, open that closet, take everything out, and organize it neatly. By analyzing the data and clues you may just discover significant truths about yourself. If shame or guilt or discomfort surfaces, it's important to just allow it, let it work itself through, and use it to help yourself see that you're no longer the same person you were then.

 Ask Sally I regret leaving a wonderful man many years ago and now find myself with someone who has none of his fine qualities. What do I do about it?—*Lily*

DEAR LILY: This fantasy is double trouble and just digs you deeper into that stuck place. Accept that you're where you need to be. Now do your work!

Don't be like some of my clients who go back to the past and feel bad about how they functioned, when they learn something new about themselves or gain insight into their behavior. Making yourself wrong for learning something new will definitely block your graduation to wisdom-hood. It's necessary to understand that you were not able to be different, that your choices in the past were based on what you knew then. Everything you learn about life and all the ways you evolve and grow can become the means for understanding your past behavior. Let these excursions into your past memories be positive ones. Celebrate your new knowledge and praise your growth, rather than negatively judging your younger, less conscious self.

Tolerate Bad Feelings

Mattie acted out sexually as a teenager and is now ashamed of her behavior. It was accepted that she would be sexually active when she was young and Mattie's mother took her to get birth control pills when she was just fourteen. Mattie says, "I look back and see that I was a smart and pretty girl, but had such low self-esteem. Those awful sexual encounters where I basically let boys use me only added to my feelings of worthlessness. I wanted love and mistakenly thought that having those guys desire me was it."

Be Your Inner Child's Mentor

1   Imagine your child self at a difficult time in the home
where you lived. See how she coped as a child in those
circumstances. As the adult that you are now, feel the
compassion for your child self and the extraordinary
hardship she endured.

2   Tell your child self or write her a letter explaining the things
you would want her to know about what she is going
through. Explain how the pain and problems that seem so
overwhelming will be resolved and tell her that, through the
process, she'll become someone admirable and resilient.
Help her understand that there is a gift, asset, or benefit
that she received from everything she has overcome.

3   Identify those hard-won gifts from your early wounding.
Conclude by saying to yourself, *I love you for how hard you
tried, for the good intentions in your heart, and especially
for your courage now.*

I helped Mattie to allow those feelings and accept that her past is a part of what helped her get to the place where she is now. No one can remake history. You can only be there to support and love yourself, seeing your choices as the best you knew at the time. When you condemn yourself, make yourself wrong, or refuse to understand your motivations you reenact the critical parent who may still live in you. Instead, work things through by tolerating your bad feelings and memories, and do for yourself what your parents were not able to do for you.

As you'll discover, the difficulties from a painful childhood—when used constructively—can empower you and provide the strength of character that can serve you well later in life. Initially, however, the deficits we have when we arrive at adulthood make it challenging to get on with the business of finding a mate, launching a career, and establishing ourselves. Mistakes that we make along the way, sometimes with disastrous consequences, are huge and wonderful learning opportunities that help us ultimately to see where to take the next step.

Grow from Your Relationship Experiences

There is currently a cultural bias against having too many relationships, marriages, and divorces. Typically, my clients are reluctant to acknowledge the number of sexual and romantic liaisons they've had. Some report that a prospective partner may want a confessional about who and how many before committing to a long-term relationship or marriage. Don't fall for this. It's rarely a good idea to come clean with anyone except your therapist. This isn't about being secretive. It's about honoring your privacy. If, as a child, you were ill prepared for relationships, the only way

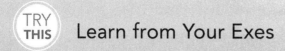

TRY THIS — Learn from Your Exes

1 Look back over your adult life and name the significant relationships that you have had.

2 Beside each relationship, identify the good things about these men, the value of the time spent with them, what you were looking for, and the things that you learned from the relationship.

3 Identify the deficits in your own character that the relationship exposed, the problems you had as a result of your own conditioning and background, and what part you played in the relationship ending.

4 Knowing what you know now, what would you have done differently in each situation?

5 End this exercise by silently thanking each relationship for furthering your understanding and growth and thanking yourself for learning what you needed to learn from each one.

to learn about life, yourself, and how to be successful in a relationship is to explore relationships, perhaps a lot of them.

 I am a regular actress and have lots of masks for different people and situations. How do I come clean and be me?—*Ginger*

DEAR GINGER: Face your anxiety about rejection and be gentle with yourself. Just recognizing this trait takes courage. Pay attention to how inauthentic it feels to role-play until you can't do it anymore.

It can be useful to study and track where you've come from and how you've evolved into a person who is better able to relate with a partner, and, even more important, with yourself—this is the basis for all relationships. Without a good connection with the deepest, most essential part of our being, relating to others can be problematic. When you know for sure that you are complete, whole, loveable, and loved, you won't need to get reinforcement from others.

Healthy Self-Interest

Mattie realized that, as a child, her feelings were not wanted and her needs were not considered. Now she's discovering that she can express that part of herself, not always, and not well, but she's getting comfortable saying what she feels and asking for what she wants. Like Mattie, you may discover that what's missing in your relationships is you. You may act from the belief that to be loved, valued, and wanted you have to take care of other people's needs and be what they want, abandon yourself, go underground, and deny yourself. Unfortunately, you may have gotten the message in childhood that it's wrong to be selfish. Oftentimes, healthy self-interest is confused with selfishness, but the two are actually quite different. Learning about what you need and like, appreciating your strengths and abilities, spending time pursuing your interests and satisfactions, and even recognizing your shortcomings are very valuable things.

Consider YOUR Mindset There is evidence that the left brain, or analytical mind, is judgmental, critical, and views yourself and others in a small and limited way. However, the right brain can view your place in the greater world as whole and complete and your true essence as connected to a bigger picture.

As a mature adult, your developmental task is to evolve into a person who is conscious and grounded in this larger experience, who can accept others as they are without demanding that they change to meet your unresolved childhood needs. You aren't the insecure person you thought you were but you are a whole, complete, beautiful being in harmony with the biggest energy that you can imagine. Without your limited thoughts about yourself, you can feel the confidence and freedom of not requiring constant reassurance to feel good about yourself. This is the place of wisdom-hood that you're moving toward. For now, you may only visit this place briefly, but eventually you will be able to take up residence on a full-time basis.

Share YOUR Views *Discuss this chapter in your book club or women's circle, or with friends:*

1 What have you learned from relationships? Compare the experiences of women who married a childhood boyfriend with others who have had a succession of relationships. What has helped you learn about yourself and your partners?

2 Draw some parallels between your childhood experiences with parents and the issues in your relationship today. What are the differences and similarities?

3 Do you think that love has to be earned, that you have to pretend to be what men want in order to be loved? What is at risk if you stop faking it?

CHAPTER 3

THOUGHTS THAT WOUND AND KILL

When a woman recognizes how her thought patterns affect everything—her moods, feelings, and behavior—it can be life-changing. The human mind is powerful and imagining something disturbing, like your man having an affair, can cause the same kind of anxiety, low energy, upset, and depression that would be present if it had actually occurred. On the other hand, believing in your own beauty and competence can imbue you with a glow of confidence that will ignite opportunities of every kind. Learning to identify your thoughts and how they affect every aspect of your life and relationship, and acquiring the skills to manage them, will be enormously empowering for you.

When you can take a more objective view of your thinking mind and are not wedded to believing everything it creates, you'll develop an expanded awareness that allows for more understanding and broader viewpoints. You'll recognize the way the mind can consume vast amounts of energy while identifying problems, evaluating people and situations, creating fearful future scenarios, reliving past regrets, and complaining about uncontrollable events, making you feel stuck and powerless. If you take the time to apply the ideas and practice using the tools discussed in this chapter, you'll be rewarded with mental clarity, greater peace, and a feeling of centeredness in your everyday life.

Don't Let Your Mind Control You

Many women have untamed minds. Their sensitive intuitive nature picks up every nuance and subtle gesture and their undisciplined mind attaches all kinds of meaning to it—some good, but much of it scary or even outrageous. Even if your mind has been educated and is accomplished in many practical functions, it may be given to leaps of fancy and extravagant associations in the relationship area. For most of us this begins in childhood when our strong need to be loved and cared for makes us enormously sensitive to other people and their moods and feelings. If you had a troubled household, or an angry, abusive father like I did, being hyper-vigilant was an important survival mechanism, a way to avoid being hurt. However, what worked well—sensing moods and feelings—in this early time of my life, became my undoing at a later time. I constantly scanned my environment and people for things that could go wrong and my mind manufactured all the frightening possibilities that might happen. I became distrusting and fearful and, because life is so difficult and unsatisfying when we fill our heads with thoughts like this, I ended up feeling chronically depressed.

Can you see how you may be allowing your rowdy mind to run your life? However, you do have a choice in the matter. You don't have to continuously believe everything your mind tells you.

Don't Believe All of Your Thoughts

The mistake I made, and that you may make, was believing my thoughts. Do you think that if you feel anxious and imagine something bad happening that the danger is real? Do you pick up on someone's stress or irritability, take it personally, and believe they don't like you? Do you assume that you can figure out other people's motives and feelings by analyzing what they say or do? Do you project your own ideas onto someone else and believe it came from them? Usually this kind of overthinking results in negative conclusions and I am constantly amazed at the innovative ways our minds have for making us miserable.

 I'm afraid that if I don't beat up my guy and myself about everything we will become fat, lazy, and unmotivated. Isn't it good to see what's wrong?—*Kayley*

> DEAR KAYLEY: That's a common but distorted belief that steals more energy than it creates. Instead, reward your efforts with affirmations and enjoy how that feels.

You may believe your thoughts are helping you when, in reality, they're hurting you. I know that when I continued to use the outdated defense mechanisms I employed as a child, I only felt disconnected and unhappy. What we focus on attracts more of the same. It isn't a secret that you get good at what you practice and, if you continuously think negative thoughts, you'll only make a wreck of yourself and your world.

Consider and Challenge Your Thoughts

If you're like Tiffany, it may not occur to you that your thoughts about your partner or your relationship may not be accurate or even true. Now thirty-two years old, Tiffany was in middle school when her mother met a man and abandoned the family, leaving behind Tiffany, her dad, and her little brother. Because of this, Tiffany has abandonment issues. When she miscarried after seven weeks of pregnancy, she was convinced her husband Blade didn't care. She says, "After the miscarriage he wasn't upset. He said something like "it probably wasn't meant to be," and then wanted to go study for his math exam. I couldn't believe how cold he was, how indifferent to what I was going through. It makes me question if I even want to be with this guy."

Thoughts like Tiffany's can trigger anger, anxiety, and depression and can interrupt the closeness, connection, and good feelings in being together. The lesson that I hope to convey to Tiffany—and to you—is that you shouldn't believe everything you think. Just because you think something doesn't make it true. There are many different ways to look at something and you rarely see the whole picture, which makes it essential that you learn to question and challenge the wild thoughts and beliefs that automatically pop up in your head due to your past conditioning.

Thoughts Cause Emotions and Behaviors

Thoughts are continual, and their function is to protect you and help you navigate through the complex world. However, when you evaluate and define yourself, your partner, and your relationship by these thoughts and believe literally what your thoughts tell you—*He's a jerk. I'm a fool to put up with this. I'm so depressed. My relationship is a disaster. This isn't working*—you allow your thoughts to create a chain of emotions and behaviors that help to bring about the very situation you want to avoid.

Emotions stem from thoughts. Women react emotionally not to what happens but to the meaning they give it in their minds. Pay attention to that last idea. It's an important one to understand. Because women have intense emotions, they often believe that their feelings inform their thoughts. They erroneously look to their feelings to guide them. The thought process goes like this: If I'm feeling hurt, then somebody did something to hurt me. If I'm feeling anxious, something bad is happening. If I'm feeling fat, I must be fat. This is backward. The correct idea to keep in mind is this one: My emotions and feelings occur in response to what I am thinking—the spin I give to what happens.

Recognize Your Thoughts and Emotions

Something triggers a particular thought—a memory, what your man said, some random event—and you wrap it up in your own packaging and believe your resulting feelings. The good news is that your mind is the best place for problems like this to be. Usually they can be solved without a lot of hard physical work and money. It just takes some time and a desire to do it.

For example, Tiffany took Blade's reaction, viewed it through the lens of her abandonment issues and memories of rejection, and naturally felt hurt and angry, which ended in a complete melt down. To help her identify some of the thought patterns and belief systems that caused her to be upset about Blade and the relationship, Tiffany agreed to keep a thought and feeling diary.

Tiffany's chart looks like this:

Date/Time	Emotion	Trigger	Thought
4/12 2:15 P.M.	Drop in energy- feel depressed at supermarket	Saw cute baby, want to have a baby	Blade may not be right partner to have it with.
4/13 5:00 P.M.	Feel hurt, rejected	Blade turned on TV when I was talking to him	He's not interested in me, I bore him.
4/13 9:00 P.M.	Angry, distant	Blade wants to make love	He only wants me for sex.
4/14 8:00 A.M.	Sad, worried	Enjoying sunny kitchen	If our marriage doesn't make it we can't keep this house.
4/14 11:00 A.M.	Suspicious, cautious	Blade left loving message on voicemail	I'm not sure I can trust him. Does he mean it?

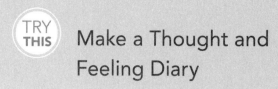

TRY THIS

Make a Thought and Feeling Diary

Organize a chart to make a thought and feeling diary for yourself. Keep a small notebook or an index card handy. When you have a change in mood—let's say things seem okay, then something happens and you feel angry, troubled, upset, worried, or any other emotional reaction you consider negative—make an entry on your chart. Note the time and day, your emotional response, and what triggered your mood change. Then see if you can identify the thought—usually an evaluation, a prediction, or the meaning of what happened. This will show you that there are only a few thoughts—your core issues—that keep repeating. If you can discover those few repetitive thought patterns, you'll be halfway to having a well-behaved, serene mind.

When Tiffany returned, I complimented her on how well she identified her thoughts, which can be difficult because we're used to having them as background noise. It usually takes practice to recognize how our mind interacts with our emotions because things other than our relationships can trigger our emotions. They can be triggered when we're alone and even simple things can cause our mood to dive. Clients tell me that putting on an outfit that doesn't look right, burning something on the stove, or getting lost while driving can cause them to view these events as resulting from their own inadequacies and they become irritable and upset. Whole days can be lost when everyday occurrences cause the mind to go off into frenzied conclusions that destroy energy. However, there are some useful tools for working with your thoughts.

Useful Tools

One of the most powerful ways to change your mood is to challenge the thoughts that created it. When you are able to identify the thought responsible for a negative emotion and consider other ways of viewing the situation, you are no longer at the mercy of your feelings and the behaviors that emanate from them. By working with your thoughts you'll be able to choose more empowering, supportive ones and reject the ones that play havoc with your mood. It will be necessary to recognize that there is a part of you that can watch your thoughts and not automatically accept them. You can learn to detach from your thinking mind and observe your thoughts with interest and make choices about which ones are useful. Later we will discuss meditation and mindfulness as other helpful practices to expand this ability.

Separate *You* from Your Thoughts

Demonstrate to yourself that you are not your thoughts. It can be useful to detach from your thinking mind. By focusing on your breath and centering yourself in your body, you can identify this space. Take a few minutes to follow your breath all the way into your body and out again several times and sense your own presence that is apart from thinking. You may even use the words *I am not my thoughts. I am more than my thinking mind.* Now look at your thoughts and create a new intention. What is it that you want in this moment? Say, *I am releasing this thought and the feelings that go with it, as it does not serve my greater good. I choose peace.*

Discover Motivations for Negative Thoughts

Another tool is to view your thought as only one of several ways to see a situation; consider other possible options. When

Tiffany looked at her thoughts, she began to see a pattern of negativity for even neutral or positive events. When she studied this more closely, she started to understand that a fear of feeling good or being too happy lay underneath the negativity. Tiffany says, "I'm worried that if I am too happy, I may jinx it or not be able to handle it if the worst happens." Tiffany felt that looking for the dark side of things would prepare her, so she wouldn't be blindsided like when she was a kid and her mother left the family. Scanning for the negative in a situation cost Tiffany a lot in bad feelings, low moods, and ultimately unhappiness.

Separate the Thought from the Thinker

A newer version of cognitive therapy called Acceptance and Commitment Therapy or ACT offers a process of labeling thoughts as a way of separating the thought from you, the thinker. I asked Tiffany to preface her thoughts using this labeling technique and say, *"A thought is occurring* . . . that our relationship may not make it. *I am having the feeling of* . . . sadness and worry." By doing this, Tiffany considers the thought or feeling as separate from herself and avoids becoming joined with it. She can be interested and curious about the thought but may not immediately bond with it. It's when we identify with our thoughts that we get lost in their creative delusions and erroneous beliefs.

Stop Evaluating Everything

Many of our thoughts are not about what's right, but about what's wrong with everything. Our intentions are good since we believe that by identifying what's problematic and what needs to be fixed we can make the problem better or set them right. It doesn't actually work that way. When you think about your

Unhook from Your Thoughts

1   Use the information you have identified in your thought and feeling diary and separate yourself by prefacing each one with the phrase, *I am having the feeling of* _____, *or I am having the thought that* _____. Notice how you are able to disassociate with that thought or feeling.

2   Look at your thought and feeling chart and consider all the different thoughts that a person could have in similar circumstances and the resulting emotions.

partner's faults and flaws, even if you don't talk about them to him or to your friends, there is the greatest likelihood that it's affecting you negatively. Consider the effect on you when you're silently ruminating on your man's words or behavior and believing that it isn't right for him to say or do those things.

Ask Sally   I get hung up on the idea that my perceptions and beliefs are true. Why do I have to make everyone else, including my boyfriend, wrong?—*Elizabeth*

DEAR ELIZABETH: Maybe you were taught that mistakes in your childhood were not okay. Now, as an adult, it's up to you to accept your flaws. Vulnerability is more attractive than perfection anyway.

Such internal thoughts and self-talk affect your mood, decrease your energy, compromise your sleep, create anxiety, interrupt your pleasure in being with your man, and may eventually drive you into therapy where you will pay a lot of money for someone to tell you what I'm telling you now. Can you be aware of how your partner is behaving or what life is handing you at a particular moment and let that be okay for now? Can you resist making it into something bad? You don't need to be on your own case either, reminding yourself about your personal defects or continuously flooding your mind with problems regarding your home, friends, and job.

Resistance Makes It Worse

The rationale behind this technique is that, in those cases where you have no control over what happens, your very act of resistance gives it energy and makes the situation worse. By stilling your judgmental self and allowing things to be as they are you'll find yourself grounded in a more serene place. Remember the mantra you were practicing in Chapter 1: *Let him be as he is.* You may like this variation: *Let it be as it is.* Making constant judgments about things that happen and reacting to them takes energy away from the more important things in life and rarely yields the positive outcomes you want. As you practice awareness without judging, you'll get better at it and come to realize that resistance to life as it unfolds is a downer that you don't need any more.

Reduce Judgment

I asked Tiffany to go back to the night when she and Blade had the big blow-up and describe his behavior without her judgments. She said, "Blade appeared calm and composed. He didn't respond to my emotion, but said something logical about the miscarriage like *it's for the best* and focused on his need to study for a final exam." I explained that the reason for the exercise was to distance herself from her evaluations and judgments and

Observe Without Judgment

For three days, be an objective observer and note every contact you have with your man without judging it. In the first column enter the date and time. In the second describe what happened in neutral terms. In the third column indicate your initial reaction and, finally, in the fourth column see if you can come up with other possible reactions. This exercise will challenge what may be a biased version of events and will help you consider other viewpoints.

to look at the situation without that filter; there may be other explanations for the same behavior. Removing judgment helps you to see that your perception of events cannot always be taken at face value. You may not be seeing the whole picture; your mind may be putting things together in novel ways that may not be accurate or true.

When witnesses are reporting on something they observed—like a crime or a car accident—there are frequently as many different aspects of the event as there are witnesses; each person may view the same thing in a different way based on their early life experiences or worldview. Also, consider that just because you're aware of a problem doesn't mean that it's a problem for everyone. It may also not be your role to solve it or offer a solution, and it may take care of itself in time without your intervention.

Negative Thoughts Have Consequences

Statistics show that while people are overwhelmingly positive about individual counseling and report an 80 to 90 percent

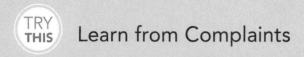

Learn from Complaints

1   What has been your experience with sharing your negative feelings with a spouse?

2   Did the behavior change for the short term? Was it effective in making permanent changes?

3   What have you discovered in your own life that is a useful approach to asking for a behavioral change?

satisfaction rate, the reverse is true of traditional marriage counseling. Some studies report that most couples who go to marriage counseling find that it is of limited value or actually makes their relationship worse. Even many of the couples who report positive responses to counseling end up divorcing. Research has shown that when couples think their problem is communication, learning how to talk and listen to each other rarely improves the relationship.

It's natural and logical to think that if you're having a problem or if something is making you stressed, unhappy, or angry, that the solution is to tell the person causing your problem to stop what they are doing. However, if you are or have been in a relationship you're probably acutely aware that sharing your negative evaluations with a partner won't necessarily improve the situation and may even make it a lot worse. Even business organizations are discovering that personnel evaluations focusing on negative performance result in low morale and are not as effective as those that emphasize positive contributions and strengths. Every successful behavior modification intervention reinforces the desired outcome, rather than focusing on the problem.

Ask for What You Want

Many women feel getting a certain something from their guy—especially if he figures out that they needed it on his own—speaks of a higher quality of love. This, of course, is a thought—a belief system—that creates your feelings and reactions. You can let this belief go as well and let love come to you from all sources and in all ways.

For example, when Tiffany looked at her reaction to Blade and imagined a different approach, she came up with some new insights. She says, "I realize I could have asked him for what I wanted without expecting him to know what I needed. It could be that he didn't recognize the depth of my pain. He's a guy. It didn't happen in his body." Tiffany thought of other ways she could have handled the situation, like calling a girlfriend, but decided that she wanted Blade to be the one to comfort her, that it would have meant more to her if he had given up his plans to stay with her.

I personally advocate that you resist the urge to criticize or share negative thoughts about your partner. Instead, use "blameless relating"—the idea that virtually everything people do is innocent and comes from an unevolved or unconscious place; there is nothing to blame, nothing to forgive, in either ourselves or others.

It's not that you can't point out what is problematic, but you should do it in a way that recognizes that the problem comes from an immature or regressed place. Isn't that what every woman truly wants—an intimate partner who so loves, accepts, and understands her that he sees everything she says and does as symptomatic of her process, and not with malicious intentions? By making your home safe from criticism, there is the distinct possibility that each of you will enjoy a deep level of self-acceptance and feel more open to sharing intimate feelings and realizations about yourself, your life, and your mate. In this climate of love, respect, and acceptance you'll be more likely to look at your own behaviors and take the steps necessary to change those things that are important to you.

Change Yourself

There is an enormous amount of power in changing yourself. If you change the way you behave in this relationship, there is a great likelihood that your partner will change as well. However, don't do it for that reason or you are giving to get, meaning that your intentions are manipulative and that you are doing something different for the purpose of changing him. It would be the same intention as nagging, just a different ploy. So carry out what you decide to do with clarity and purity of heart, because it's what you choose for your growth and because it creates the peace and acceptance you believe is important for yourself. If you lead by example and he follows it's a happy byproduct.

Consider Acceptance

You may want your partner to change and treat you with love and appreciation—the way you may not have been cared for as a child. However, you are likely to feel disappointment or pain in the event that your partner can't be the parent you didn't have. When you're upset and your first response is to blame your partner, consider changing yourself instead and just feeling hurt or disappointed and not making him wrong. Acknowledge that you didn't get what you wanted, that your needs aren't being fulfilled, or that you feel lonely, but accept the situation for what it is without putting pressure or expectations on your partner to make it better. Consider that you don't know what it is like to actually be your partner with his heredity, background, upbringing, experiences, and so forth, and that your mind may just be assuming that it knows how he should think, feel, or behave in any given situation.

It isn't necessary to try to rationalize your partner's responses. Just allow the reaction to be appropriate for him and don't attempt to encourage or shape him to meet your expectations.

Ask Sally I want my guy to read my moods and feelings, know what I need, and then give it to me without my having to ask him. What's wrong with that?—Wendy

DEAR WENDY: Very few men are able or willing to provide this and trying to get it will cause a lot of conflict and pain for you.

Consider YOUR Mindset You might discover that, by giving your partner and relationship the space to *be*, that there are good and valuable discoveries to be made. You can learn and benefit from being open to different ideas and viewpoints. In the process, you'll discover that you have a lot more control over your once untamed mind, that it now functions as an accurate and trusted servant and can stay peacefully present but not intrusive. It will eventually accept that it doesn't run the show and doesn't always have the answers.

Discuss this chapter in your book club or women's circle, or with friends:

1 How easy has it been for you to identify your thoughts and beliefs and start to change them? Have you discovered that there are reoccurring thoughts that pop up frequently?

2 Consider your tendency to look at problems and consider what needs to be fixed. What do you think will happen, for good or bad, if you reverse this trait and see the positives?

3 Do you see value in becoming more accepting of your partner even if he doesn't reciprocate and give you the same in return?

CHAPTER 4

STUCK IN STICKY STORIES

Everyone loves stories—novels, vignettes from history, a bit of news about a neighbor. We even weave our own stories—fun tales about meeting our spouse or memories of our children's cute ways. However, as disappointment and pain settle into a relationship, stories with a distinctly dark side emerge and gather reinforcement. For example, you may create stories that negatively describe your partner and discuss how he became that way. Then, once you become invested in these labels and stories, you test your partner to gather more data—and prove your point.

If you were stereotyped by others or created a story about yourself that was limiting, you know how labels can thwart your growth. Even exaggerated positive descriptions can be uncomfortable to live with. So, learn to see the whole picture and our fluid changing personalities and let go of the stories that create misery for yourself.

How Women View the Truth

Most women love the game of molding reality. The truth is usually very elastic for us, just like a comfy pair of yoga pants that fit no matter how our shape changes; or like a scrapbook, where a miserable rainy vacation at the beach looks wonderful when all the pictures with catchy phrases are pasted on the page. Because we connect with people by sharing the things that happen and how we're feeling about our life's events, our stories may be embellished, exaggerated, or slanted a particular way . . . especially if they create excitement, amusement, or interest in our audience. After all, it's fun and no one expects everything we say to be the unvarnished truth. Men may suggest that women lie, but they don't understand our nature when they frame it that way. Because women are focused on connection and relationship and revel in sharing both themselves and their viewpoints with the special people in their lives, their truth will be packaged with the unique shape they give it—just like those stretch pants.

Words Have Staying Power

As a woman whose essence is life giving, you create with your being, your consciousness, and even more so with what you say. You set the tone and the mood, work magic with your beautiful energy, and light up a room with your presence. You also realize that words are your most damaging weapon when you want to carry out the feminine version of war. When you're wounded and hurting and refuse to accept your powerlessness to change a situation, you may use them to at least get even. The stories you tell at these times are not innocent stories. Rather, they're toxic ones that may cause damage that can never be undone.

The things you say can have enormous power and, if said often enough, can build a convincing case with far-reaching effects. If your thoughts are potent, then your words are packed with even more ammunition as they establish and reinforce beliefs and patterns in a relationship.

Resist Making Up Stories

I challenged Ella to look at the stories she was telling her mother and friends about her husband Jeff. I refused to accept her version of him. She was painting him as a passive, lazy, unmotivated guy who was letting life pass him by. She says, "I know he struggles with his job and where he wants his career to go. He has a lot of self-esteem issues too, but he's actually a good dad. But remember, when Jeff proposed to me eight years ago he didn't even have enough money to buy me the ring—I had to put it on my card. Now, we're bursting out of this rented duplex—we need a bigger house. I want him to get going!" Do you find it curious that Ella married a guy who couldn't afford a ring, but still believes she can remake him into a go-getter in the business world? Do you think some of her old personal issues are being activated here?

 I pretend to my family and girlfriends that my man is perfect and make up stories that show him off. What's wrong with that?—*Theresa*

DEAR THERESA: Who are you really trying to convince? By facing the normal disappointment in relationships you can grow in maturity and acceptance rather than continuing to tell a story.

Stories Grow and Evolve

Stories like those Ella tells usually have a central protagonist—a guy, with a certain personality and behaviors. Frequently the characters created are mysteriously like other people from the past—a parent or an ex. There's a plot line that fits this character and, when there are obstacles or problems, he makes decisions in keeping with his personality, which propel the story forward. As entertainment in a movie or a novel, character-driven adventures are fun. But, if you're describing your partner in this way, you're putting him in a box and creating a concept of who he is. Your mind becomes invested in these characteristics and you start to see things contributing to the story and building evidence, making the ideas stick together into a cohesive narrative.

Ella troubled her friends and family with her own fears that Jeff wasn't working hard enough, wasn't getting ahead at work, was shunning responsibility, and wasn't going to get them out of debt and into their own home. She kept them up to date with each new chapter: *You won't believe what happened. You'll never guess what he did.* Ella's own anxieties were the driving force for her story.

Stories Affect Everyone

You distance yourself from your man when you disparage him to your friends. Speaking badly about your mate betrays him, just as putting yourself down betrays you. It's disloyal and violates the trust you have with each other. Ella discovered that one outcome to weaving negative stories about Jeff and their relationship was the effect on her mood. When she was complaining to her mother, she noticed that she didn't feel close to or affectionate with him, but went home anxious and worried about their future together. Even Jeff remarked that she seemed quiet and far away.

I was curious to see if Ella had some insight about why she felt it necessary to reveal the problems Jeff was having even if she believed what she said. She replied, "I think I'm angry with him. I bring these matters up to him and he doesn't do anything, so I get even by ratting on him to his mother, my mother, everyone!" Making Jeff look bad is how Ella gets back at Jeff, but I asked her to consider the effect it has on her. "I must look bad, too, for being with this guy I make out to be a loser. It doesn't help our relationship either." Ella was right. Creating negative stories with

TRY THIS Separate from Your Story

Identify three stories you have about your partner and preface each with this phrase: *I'm creating the story that* _____. Now practice separating yourself from your stories. Again, having a thought or idea and believing it as a truth are not one and the same. We can choose to believe it or we can choose not to. Only if we are conscious of having a choice can we exercise one.

potentially bad outcomes is an extension of your thinking and it has the same effect on your feelings, mood, and behavior. It's impossible to craft negative stories and not feel anxious, ambivalent, irritated, or depressed.

When you recognize you're doing this to yourself or to your partner, it's important to separate yourself from the story. When Ella said, *I am creating a story that Jeff is not making a financially secure future for us* it felt different than when she said *Jeff is not making a financially secure future for us*. In the first case she could label it as a story rather than accept it as a fact.

Risks in Sharing Stories

You may be asking: *These people I talk to are my trusted support group. Am I not supposed to confide in them, get help from them?* The answer is no. If you tell your stories repeatedly to close friends and family, they will take on your beliefs about your man and help to reinforce your conceptualization. Since you know your guy better than they do, your friends will rarely challenge your beliefs. In fact, they may even enjoy your revelations. Some women tell me that it comforts them to know others have relationship problems, or that they feel better when a woman they envy acknowledges painful realities about her life. When you are feeling negative or angry with your partner, these ideas are likely to stick with your confidants. Then, on a good day when you are feeling more positive, they may not easily release the bad feelings they harbor about him. Can you see how this is a dangerous path to go down? For those of you who have lived this dilemma, you know that life can get uncomfortable straddling the different social situations where you've said things that may come back to bite you.

Don't Play the Right and Wrong Game

We discussed how anxiety and resentment may push women to reveal too much, but there's another motivation to portray your man in a bad light: you get to feel superior. You've seen the ads or sitcoms where the goofball guy has a patient but condescending wife. That's not you, is it? This is a theme that appeals to many women for obvious reasons. When this is the theme of your stories, you have to ask what you get out of that belief system. Do you like the idea that women are the superior gender and men are inept, pathetic, and lost without us? This tactic doesn't build up a guy in a way that commands your respect. It doesn't make him seem confident, sexy, or like someone you would find attractive. But it does keep you more guarded and less emotionally available.

 I always thought women were superior, seriously. You mean those jokes were wrong?—*Paula*

DEAR PAULA: Some women are more comfortable in relationships where they are clearly the boss. Appreciate his willingness to play beta to your alpha.

No One Likes Labels

You may know something about being stereotyped. Maybe you were considered independent, shy, or rebellious and stories were repeated that supported those conceptualizations—perhaps to the point where you believed those things about yourself. Your relatives may still see you in the same way even now that you're an adult and may say things like, *You were always willful and determined. Cried a lot. Good at math.* Whatever the story, it is only one tiny facet of you if it's true at all. Saying things aloud repeatedly embeds these ideas and colors your view of a person or of an event.

You Are More Than a Story

I used to have well-rehearsed stories that I told when I met new friends or lovers; stories that portrayed me the way I wanted to appear. I described how my life choices shaped me into what I wanted people to believe about me and the stories were slanted to elicit a positive response. Over time, these carefully constructed stories became my reality. I came to believe them myself. I had lost track of the details I didn't want to remember and emphasized the things I liked about my journey. I became my story.

It's a trap to craft yourself this way, but it's even worse to reinforce negative beliefs about yourself. I've had enumerable clients say negative and demeaning things about themselves: *There's nothing I do well. I wonder why anyone would want me for a friend. I am not at all attractive.* Some women use one-liners to put themselves down: *I'm a klutz. I can't cook. I have bad luck.* These one-liners are a distortion, an exaggeration of one aspect of yourself. Every time you repeat this story you embed it more deeply into your belief system, which affects your energy and mood.

You are a complex person who is constantly growing and evolving. There isn't any story that can describe you, no concept that can define you. Release yourself right this minute from every negative idea you have believed about yourself. Promise to stop yourself when these old labels surface. Instead, say something affirming like: *I am free of labels.* Print that mantra in your day planner, on sticky notes, or on a ribbon for your wrist so you never forget.

How Women Test Men

As part of her story-making, Ella found she was frequently testing Jeff. She had a belief or hypothesis about him—that he wasn't interested in getting ahead. She would give him job ads from the newspaper or bring up conversations about companies that were hiring when they were out with friends. When Jeff didn't follow through on these leads, he flunked the test, and Ella concluded that she was right about him—that he was lazy and unmotivated.

There are all kinds of tests, some more subtle than Ella's. Most of the tests are to determine if he truly cares. Will he remember important dates if you don't remind him? If you're pouting in the bedroom will he find out what you're upset about? Will he notice the new blouse you're wearing? Many women offer their partners the opportunity to do something they want to do. Have you ever said something like: *Just relax and watch your program, I'll do the dishes,* or: *It's okay if you want to go out with the guys, I don't mind?* This is a setup if you don't honestly mean what you say. You're testing him to see if he truly loves you, wants to be with you, and prefers you over another favorite activity. Of course, most men won't realize it's a test and, when your guy flunks, you get to feel disappointed and have more evidence to add to your story. This game isn't fun for either of you and it only means what you decide it means. There is no empirical evidence that the test is valid or measures what you intend.

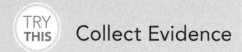

TRY THIS   Collect Evidence

1   What are the stories you tell yourself or others about your partner or relationship? Take a minute to write down those stories. Do you tell stories of events or incidents that portray him in a certain way or explain the way he is? Finish these sentences:

- My husband is a man who _____.

- He would be better if he didn't _____.

- I find his _____ difficult to tolerate.

- I want him to _____.

2   How do you collect evidence that reinforces your beliefs and helps you create the story?

3   How do you test your partner, to gather evidence that he is this way?

Men's Typical Responses

Men report that they have three bad choices when their women pressure them to do something. The first is to do what you want, which makes him feel like a kid or an employee. The second choice is to resist your pressure, which makes him feel stronger and more like his own person, but he knows he'll get more anger and insistence from you as a result. Finally, he may respond passive-aggressively by doing it slowly or badly to get even. It's a corner with no graceful exit.

 I always thought love was a feeling and being in love was a greater feeling but how do you get or stay there?—*Brenda*

DEAR BRENDA: Emotions—including feelings of attachment, connection, warmth, and caring—come from our thoughts. Love of every kind can be blocked by negative thoughts and stories or encouraged by gratitude and appreciation.

I know what you are asking now in total exasperation: *How in the world am I going to get him to do what I want, or do anything for that matter?* The simplest way is usually the best. Ask him in a heartfelt way and let it go without all of the drama. If you don't get what you want, perhaps you'll get something better instead. You may get frustrated, but you'll also be challenged to grow in patience, acceptance, and love.

Eliminate Judging

The bottom line is that making up stories and creating a conceptualization of your partner involves judging. You decide that there is a right way for him to be or act, provide a lot of coaching to shape his behavior in that direction, and react negatively if he deviates from that program. There are some situations (for example, jobs or parenting) where this kind of evaluation is necessary and useful, but it doesn't enhance connection or closeness in the realm of intimate relationships. Emphasizing positive attributes is not a better approach as most partners don't buy the global praise such as *you're the greatest, you're brilliant,* and so on. It is possible to notice things about your partner without making them a fault or a virtue and it's appropriate to recognize the positive things he does. For example, say, *Thanks for cleaning up the kitchen. You were fun to be with tonight. I always enjoy sharing my day with you.* This kind of expression is from your heart rather than a judgment from your mind.

Consider **YOUR** Mindset True love or friendship doesn't ask anyone to be other than who or what they are. It doesn't presume to know the right way for a person to think, feel, or behave, and doesn't take on the task of attempting to fix or coach a person to become something different. It's healthier to allow others to develop in their own unique way without your interference. Of course, it's not required that you be with someone if it is not in your best interest, but acceptance is the highest calling of friendship to yourself as well as others.

Discuss this chapter in your book club or women's circle, or with friends:

1 How do stories take on a life of their own and get exaggerated and reinforced over time with each new bit of information? What would be lost if you never told stories? What innocent stories are still possible?

2 The whole idea of not judging is a hard one for many women. Consider how the judgments and labels of others have affected you.

3 Testing is something all women have done in some manner. What tests do you see as helpful? Which ones are harmful? Has your partner caught on to some tests and is too savvy now to play?

CHAPTER 5

AVOIDING PAIN CREATES MORE

In our quest for the perfect existence we can be baffled about how to handle the pain of life. As women, we may try to control the emotions that threaten our happiness. However, unlike physical pain that alerts us to what is wrong, some psychic pain is a natural part of being human and can't be eliminated. It must be accepted and allowed until it resolves on its own. This is certainly true in relationships, where much of the pain that women experience originates. Suffering, which is different from pain, occurs when you resist the normal flow of positive and negative experiences and feelings and attempt to have only the ones you want.

Feelings Give Information

Your body houses all your feelings. The subtle sensations you experience here are an important source of information as they tell you how your mind is interpreting events. Your body is the home of amazing sensory pleasures as well as happiness and joy. Intuition and gut instincts reside here. Women are socialized to be sensitive and empathic with others, and new research demonstrates that the female brain is designed with larger relationship and communication areas than the male brain. So it is a great blessing as a woman to be able to experience the full range of human emotions. Problems arise when you attempt to reduce or eliminate the normal pain and disappointment that is a part of life. As you learned in a previous chapter, painful feelings can sometimes be resolved if erroneous beliefs and irrational thoughts are the basis for these emotions. However, there are those feelings—genuine responses to events and happenings—that just are. For those feelings there is nothing to do but comfort and support yourself as they run their course.

By trying to avoid negative or painful feelings, you may make one of the three following wrong turns:

- Numb body sensations and stop recognizing feelings, both good and bad.
- Fear bad feelings like anxiety or depression and continually focus on trying to avoid or get rid of them, thereby increasing their power.
- Believe that your feelings require that someone or something needs to change to make them go away

Don't Block Your Feelings

The first mistake you can make is to numb your body sensors and stop recognizing your feelings. It's as if your body was anesthetized from the neck down and its sole purpose is to carry your head around, believing erroneously that thinking is your primary activity and feeling is of little or no value. You may know women who roleplay a perky, friendly affect but have no heart—they are missing this key link. You may be more comfortable this way but, because your feelings have been cut off, you'll only have your mind, which will respond to events in a cognitive rather than emotional way—a masculine trait. You will lose your feminine nature and become genderless, a woman who can't embody herself and who can't feel her essence, passion, or joy.

 What do you do with the ache or longing at night when you are convinced that he doesn't care?—*Shirley*

DEAR SHIRLEY: If you can't change your thoughts and find another reason for his behavior, and you can't ask him for reassurance, then allow the feelings to open you to your truth.

You may block emotions, believing that you'll be overwhelmed or unable to function if you let yourself feel them. This may happen, but it's unlikely. Maybe you learned during childhood that to survive you needed to stop feeling, or perhaps you had a difficult time enduring deep emotions earlier in your life. Some women believe that bad feelings are the antithesis of happiness and that blocking them will yield more pleasure, but paradoxically the opposite is true. You will enjoy more pleasure by allowing yourself to feel the full range of human emotions.

Blocking emotions is the primary reason people turn to addictions of every kind. Repetitive, often destructive, behaviors like gambling or substance abuse, or even more innocent versions like compulsive eating or video games have some intermittent gratification, but the overarching purpose is to distract you from the feelings you want to avoid at all costs. Every person who successfully licked an addiction will attest to the feelings that surfaced when the addicted substance or activity was gone.

Don't Fear Bad Feelings

The second wrong turn in pain management is to try to get rid of your bad feelings, which often causes them to grow and intensify because you are focusing so much attention on eliminating them. By obsessing about the feelings and wanting them gone you increase the likelihood they will get worse; this is especially true of anxiety and depression. There is no better way to strengthen the grip of your pain than to be unwilling to feel it and try to fight it off. It's like getting rid of a no-good lover. He will stick like fly paper, show up when you're most vulnerable and lonely, and, despite your objections, get a perverse satisfaction from romancing you into bed one more time.

Perhaps you believe there is a way to eliminate negative feelings that you haven't discovered and you want the tools that will do the job once and for all. Identifying your thoughts and reworking and challenging the erroneous ones are the best ways to improve negative moods but, as we discussed earlier, emotions must often be tolerated and managed—not eliminated. I'm sorry to disappoint you when I tell you that the only way to stop fearing bad feelings is to welcome them and learn to manage them. Paradoxically, the more you resist something the more it hangs around. Accepting what is—even if it's your lousy mood—will allow you to take the action necessary to change it, but rejecting and denying the painful feeling is only arguing with reality and digs you deeper into the hole of suffering.

I have seen women who develop chronic avoidance patterns in an attempt to control their bad feelings. They believe that they can reduce their exposure to anything that negatively affects their mood—be they people, places, or events. If someone upsets them at a class, they stop going. If they have a panic attack at the mall, they don't go anymore. If driving on bridges makes them nervous, they won't go anywhere that involves crossing a bridge. Instead of accepting their feelings and allowing them to be, these women give their negative feelings power. The stakes get even higher when this strategy empowers and emboldens the very feelings they are avoiding. In a vicious cycle the more these

Investigate Change Strategies

1   Identify a complaint or problem you are having with your partner. What is he doing or not doing that bugs you?

2   How do you react when you witness his behavior? What are your feelings?

3   What have you done to get him to change?

4   How effective have you been in resolving this problem and reducing your pain?

5   Did your attempts make things better or worse? Did they decrease your pain or increase your suffering?

women shrink their life, the more powerful the negative feelings become. You can see where this strategy leads you—to bed with covers over your head.

Don't Make Your Feelings His Problem

A third way of not dealing with your own pain is to make it all about your man and try to get him to fix it. Many women are stuck in the belief that their happiness is dependent on being cherished and adored by a partner and they have great difficulty taking responsibility for creating more satisfaction and pleasure for themselves. This can be a rough rollercoaster ride of emotions as daily your partner's words and behaviors will either improve or depress your mood. You may resort to all kinds of tests and manipulations. Men with this type of woman often grow weary of her neediness and tune out. Even if you escalate your demands and heighten the drama, your partner may feel unable to meet your regressed needs. As long as you look outside yourself for what you need to feel good, loved, or complete, the more suffering you'll cause yourself and your partner.

Pain: A Necessary Part of Life

Especially in relationships there are no guarantees, no happily-ever-after promises. Relationships are all about risk and adventure. You throw yourself, your emotions, and your heart into what you hope will be a source of joy, love, and continual blessings. Perhaps it is for a while, but eventually you'll feel the pain of disappointment, betrayal, and loss. It can't be otherwise. Life is designed to test, teach, challenge, and at times torment you. That's just how it is. If you shorten your emotional range by blocking bad feelings, you'll lose the good ones too. You can't have it both ways. When you avoid pain, you deaden yourself to pleasure, happiness, and joy. However, you'll learn how to reduce the suffering by fully experiencing everything—the pleasure, pain, and everything else that is happening—without resistance and by surrendering to what can't be changed.

You Can't Escape from All Pain

When your pain is intense, it's likely you'll want to escape. This is what happened with Stephanie when she and her husband, Nathan, were unable to have a baby. She began working more when her husband Nathan began gaining weight and stopped doing the physical things like biking and tennis they had both enjoyed in the early years of their marriage. She didn't want to watch him eat junk food, sit in front of the TV, and grow out of his clothes. It was easier to come home late, grab a bite after work, and not be reminded of how their lives were growing apart.

It's typical to try to make the pain go away by attempting to fix the problem. Stephanie nagged Nathan about his weight gain, begged him to work out with her, became a food cop, and tried to purge their grocery cart of the offending items, but it just made matters worse. He was hurt by her criticism, angry that she was unsympathetic to his problem, and retreated further into his comfort food.

Stephanie didn't realize that she was externalizing her pain, making Nathan the problem and, in the process, making herself a victim. In creating this belief, she was inadvertently setting up a no-win situation where her happiness was tied to Nathan changing his behavior.

"It's necessary to fully feel the pain," I told Stephanie. "When you make someone else responsible for your pain you become a victim, and then all you have is a story to explain why you are hurting. Let yourself experience the feeling you're avoiding. Feel it without attaching labels, blame, and attacks. Don't let your mind explain and resist it." Stephanie was reluctant to try this. She was afraid her feelings would be overwhelming and she wouldn't be able to handle them. She realized that she had a heavy defense system in place and it was scary to let down her guard.

 If I am always unhappy and believe that my partner's behavior is causing me to feel this way, am I being a victim?—*Danielle*

DEAR DANIELLE: Now you only see one option for yourself and that one option is not within your power to carry out. You won't be a victim if you begin to take small steps to find your own happiness.

Accept Your Pain

Stephanie eventually decided that she was willing to sit back in a recliner and experience the feeling as much as she could tolerate, as long as she could interrupt the session whenever she wanted. I asked her to describe how she feeling, to let herself know what it was that she didn't want to experience.

She said, "It's like a hole inside. A dark place. Emptiness. A place I want to get away from. It's achy. I feel lost in there." As Stephanie focused her feelings eventually a shift began to occur. She began to discover that when she stopped fighting the feeling she began to feel more comfortable with the longing that she was having. It no longer frightened her.

She remembered feeling like this as a child when her single mother who worked long hours left her in day care and at extended programs at school and summer camps. Her ambitious, intelligent mother never married, but decided at age forty that she would try for one special child, Stephanie. Her mother provided a high standard of living for their two-person family—a beautiful home, private schools—but not much in the way of other relatives, activities, or fun. There were no aunts, uncles, or cousins, only a godmother—her mother's best friend who provided the only family life she knew.

Stephanie cried as she was flooded with the emotions she had buried. She realized she was avoiding the pain in her life now the same way she had avoided pain as a child by studying hard, staying busy, and suppressing her loneliness. As a teenager she blamed her mother for leaving her alone for much of her growing up years. Today, Stephanie was blaming Nathan, shutting off her emotions by working long hours like she learned from her mother. However, this time she was lonely by her own unconscious choosing.

"I see that I believed that Nathan and a baby could fill that empty place and it's disappointing to realize that they can't." Stephanie accepted that this wouldn't be a quick fix. What I told her is what I am telling you—that when you allow yourself to be fully present and feel your feelings without denying, repressing, or medicating them, there is a greater likelihood that you can move through them rather than creating more suffering for yourself.

An Important Truth about Pain

It's important for you to learn a powerful idea that has the ability to make your journey so much smoother: Suffering is created when you try to make bad feelings go away. Look at Stephanie! She had several worthless strategies that only increased her pain and caused more suffering. She stuffed her original pain into the mental junk closet and covered it over with career ambition, lots of work, and an obsessive fitness routine. Then, when Nathan disappointed her dreams of being active together and having a family, she created more suffering by nagging and trying to reform him, which only set his passive aggression in motion.

You, like Stephanie, need to realize that both everyday pains as well as the bigger ones can throw you off course. You can churn your insides up and lose massive amounts of energy by making people wrong, attempting to fix impossible situations, stewing in resentment, and making plans to retaliate. When your partner goes golfing on Saturday and doesn't repair the pool filter like he promised, or when someone takes your parking place after you've circled the lot for twenty minutes, you can be disappointed, but these are everyday episodes. These continuous events won't stop occurring until life is over.

Recognize a Pain Bond

If you had a difficult childhood, you may have connected with your caregivers through the chaos of their problematic life and grown up believing that love and pain are interwoven. You may have unconsciously duplicated this situation as an adult by staying in a miserable, conflicted situation. Instead of resolving those important needs left over from the past, you recreate the suffering you learned as a child.

I have seen women who can keep the pain bond alive with a man even if he leaves or dies because the suffering substitutes for a real relationship. Without that energy drain, she would have to take responsibility for her own happiness and get on with her life, something that may be too threatening or overwhelming for her. She may have some distorted beliefs that keep her locked into this misery: she feels there is no one else for her, she is too damaged to move on, and so on. This lifestyle may have illness, physical pain, depression, and other kinds of adversity in it as well. If you're suffering in this way, you may require professional help to move forward.

Allow Feelings to Be

I've had clients who lament and wail in my office about some event that happened several years before. This is suffering run amok. The rationale for people who extend their suffering indefinitely is that they believe there is something they need to learn, fix, or do to make the pain go away. In most cases, they have done all of these and are still cycling back through the painful event over and over again. These people need to learn that, oftentimes, there is nothing to do but surrender to what is and accept that sometimes they are powerless to fix a situation. There is no need to talk themselves out of the feelings or blame someone else for them. They must surrender to their feelings and reactions and let them go.

 Is it always necessary to forgive people who've hurt me in the past?—*Andrea*

> DEAR ANDREA: If you keep ruminating over incidents or they ambush you when you least expect it, then there is forgiveness you need to do. Memories should come and go peacefully.

Stephanie seemed more conscious, more present with herself, when I saw her after she explored her painful memories. She agreed that facing the pain was difficult, but it was a better response than avoiding it. She reported that she is less driven to stay overly active and busy, more able to be with Nathan as he is, and more accepting of her life—both the good and bad parts—as it is. However, there are still things she definitely wants to change. I told her that making decisions from this healthier place will ultimately be a conscious choice. I'm telling you the same thing: being present, conscious, and feeling what is going on is ultimately a better place from which to make decisions and take action.

TRY
THIS

Uncover and Allow Feelings

1   See if you can get in touch with a feeling that you are
    avoiding. Use the complaint or problem with your partner
    that you identified in the exercise on page 67 or another
    feeling that you are having.

2   Ask yourself if you are willing to experience your feelings
    fully. Find a quiet spot with few distractions and let yourself
    identify the sensations, the felt sense, the internal state you
    are having. Try to avoid thinking and instead let yourself
    experience it.

3   What, if anything, shifted as a result of this experiment?

4   What did you learn in doing this exercise?

The Message Hidden in Pain

In subsequent sessions, Stephanie took more responsibility for her own happiness. She began to realize that both she and Nathan wanted things that interfered with the desires of the other. Stephanie's career was important to her. As a child she had always excelled in school and it seemed natural for her to work harder and longer hours at a job to get ahead. Family life was important to Nathan and he wanted Stephanie to relax more, watch TV with him in the evenings, and plan dinners at home. Stephanie used to punish Nathan by working late as a passive-aggressive way of dealing with her anger over his lifestyle choices but, in reality, working late was what she wanted to do anyway. Now Stephanie has started a process that Nathan has also picked up. They ask for what they want, but accept whatever they get without making the other person wrong. Each person, at times, needs to take care of themselves, but at other times give a gift to the other partner or to the relationship. They hold the notion that life involves more than being half of a couple—that each individual has dreams and goals that are independent of the life they share.

Forgiveness Is Necessary

Forgiveness is a useful tool for resolving both everyday hurts and longstanding wounds. One approach, which differs somewhat from mine, suggests that it's important to release the wrongdoer and accept that, although you were hurt by his actions or words, you're letting it go for your own healing. However, it doesn't condone what was done or absolve the person of the responsibility for what they did.

My approach is to understand that the person who hurt you was so unconscious, blocked, and immature in their evolution that they were incapable of doing better. This helped me let go of my childhood wounding at the hands of an alcoholic and abusive father. When I saw him as someone who was immature and coping with his own terrible past in a poor way, I could actually have empathy for the life he led that drove him to act out destructively. So the forgiveness did not arise from my magnanimous desire to release him from the hurt he caused our family but instead came from my acceptance that he was impaired and incapable of more. I could actually feel compassion for his suffering. You may not have had these same wounding experiences, but the way I resolved mine may show you how to work through your own issues whether the events are recent or from long ago. Both forms of forgiveness are available to you, use whichever works best.

Consider YOUR Mindset   Suffering is different from pain. Pain occurs when your needs aren't met, things don't work out successfully, or you don't receive the love and attention you crave. Suffering is what you create yourself when you are unwilling to face up to the inevitable and necessary pain in your life. You make yourself suffer when you resist the reality of your life right now, when you refuse to accept what *is*, and when you use anger and control tactics to get others to conform to your needs and expectations. You can expend huge amounts of energy lamenting and wailing, deaden yourself with addiction, or just accept that pain is a part of life.

Discuss this chapter in your book club or women's circle, or with friends:

1 What strategies have you used to manage difficult or painful feelings, especially those from a breakup or divorce?

2 How have they looked to your man to fix a situation and make the pain go away rather than accepting that it is something you need to resolve or allow to heal on its own?

3 Consider the degree of difficulty in accepting that life is always going to be a mixture of pleasure and pain. Do you believe that it's possible to avoid pain or lessen its impact?

4 How much pain have you caused yourself through your own beliefs and thoughts? Could you reduce that stress by changing your thinking?

PART TWO

THE NO-CONFLICT MINDSET

In this section, you'll learn how to reduce the conflict in your relationship and improve the connection you have with your partner. I've outlined a new vision of relationships, which I call blameless relating. It shows you how to learn about and appreciate the man you have without the overlay of your expectations and even delusions. By becoming more authentic and learning to please yourself you will be more interesting and create positive energy for him as well. When you stop trying to shape and coach your man to be what you want and practice accepting him as he is, you will be rewarded with more maturity and resilience. Empathy is a powerful skill that may have the effect of opening your man to his deeper feelings and strengthening the bond between you even if he is not able to reciprocate. As a woman who is biologically and socially shaped for relationships, you will be able to use these skills and lead by example.

CHAPTER 6

REALLY *GET* HIM

Women cause an enormous amount of conflict within themselves and in their relationship when they believe that they know how their man should be. An innocent suggestion about the best shirt to go with a tie may morph into a full-scale attempt to revise his entire personality. You may want to help, be valued, and think that what's perfect for you and your view of the world is good for him. However, pain and unhappiness only increase when you expect your partner to give up his preferences and who he *is* to be more of what you need. These expectations are the opposite of acceptance and love.

Men are highly sensitive to criticism and, even though criticism doesn't result in positive change for most people, women rely on this common tactic, which often escalates the problem. As you attempt to shape your partner into someone who can meet your demands and expectations, you may overlook the person he truly is and sabotage the very connection you seek. In many cases, women are driven by unmet needs from childhood revisited on their partners and re-wounding themselves in the process. In this chapter, you'll learn how to look at your partner without the heavy expectations that he will fulfill all your needs and how to view him through the prism of what's good about both him and the relationship instead of what's missing.

Get Out of the Way

To truly understand your man, you need to get out of the way. Seeing him in the light of how he meets your needs blocks your vision. If you're so wedded to your belief that you know how he *should* be, you'll be unable to see him in the context of his own life—how he *really* is. Having these blinders on will impede the natural flow of your relationship and will be the cause of much conflict, anger, and disconnection. Because this idea is so important to your life with your partner, I want to help you understand by giving you an analogy based on your relationship with your parents.

 If I keep trying to get my husband to see the doctor, is that caring or is that criticism?—*Anna*

DEAR ANNA: The first time you make the suggestion is caring. After that it's criticism.

Learn from Your Parents

When you were growing up, your parents may have looked at your emerging personality and envisioned how you would become as an adult. They may have had dreams of you having an outgoing personality, dressing fashionably, being popular, dancing ballet, attending their alma mater, marrying well, living nearby, and having grandchildren for them to spoil. As you grew up and formed your own ideas about your life, you may have detoured from your parents' dreams and disappointed them. You may have decided to take up competitive ping pong, drop out of college, move to China, and rescue abandoned potbellied pigs.

If your parents can embrace this different version of you and continue to support your being in the world even if it isn't what they planned for you, you may stay close. If they can't let go of their dreams and attempt to shape you to their desires, your relationship may rupture. Parents who continue to give unwanted advice to their grown children and fail to understand their dreams and values usually see them less frequently and play a smaller part in their lives. This can even work in reverse if your aging parents stubbornly refuse your advice about giving up their big house and moving to a retirement villa.

The reason I bring this up is that there is a huge tendency for people who love each other to have strong ideas about what is best for each other. To actually understand your man and see him in the context of his own life, you need to resist the urge to shape him into the person that you want him to be: the one who perfectly meets your needs or the fantasy version of him that you imagined when you were first together. Coaching and advising your man in all aspects of his life can cause a lot of conflict in a relationship. It gets in the way of you allowing your partner to have some autonomy about his life and preferences and it definitely disrupts the connection between the two of you.

Coaching and Criticism

At the beginning of your relationship, you may have tried to show your man how valuable you were by advising him about hair styling, wardrobe choices, and home décor. But what did you do when he started to bristle at your comments and defended himself against what he interpreted as criticism? *But these are my favorite sneakers* he may have said when digging them out of the garbage. Are you hurt when he rejects your ideas? Do you then see him as the cause of the conflict—a bozo, missing the boat and hopelessly out of sync? Your sense of superiority may begin when you start to portray your partner as inadequate, socially inept, or clueless. When you can't get your man to revise his personality and behavior in the ways you desire, you may defend yourself by seeing him as wrong and yourself as right. If you can't fix him, you can at least feel superior to him. However, when you do this, your man loses stature and becomes less attractive, sexy, and desirable in every way, and your ability to feel close is compromised.

When it comes down to it, it's so unnecessary to be right, argue silly points, or position yourself as an authority on anything—much less how another person should be. Allowing everyone to have their own opinions or preferences and accepting that, in most cases, there is no need for things to be right or wrong can reduce unnecessary friction with your partner. Of course, this will require you to grow and change but that's a good thing, that's the purpose of a relationship. You cannot take it personally that his hairy toes stick out of his sandals when you look hot for a night out. You can feel hurt when he falls asleep at the expensive play you arranged or just let him snooze.

Criticism Isn't Productive

No one responds well to criticism—not employees, not spouses, not children, not even dogs. Bring viewed negatively make us regress to childhood, is often deeply humiliating and hurtful, and can result in feelings of anger and resentment. Criticism usually strengthens one's defense mechanism and does not result in change. Men especially have been socialized to see their external accomplishments as indicative of their worth and are highly sensitive to negative feedback and criticism. Women, on

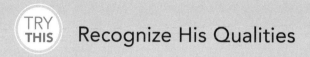

TRY THIS — Recognize His Qualities

1 What are the character traits you most admire about your partner? What hard things did he accomplish in life that helped him become the man he is?

2 What are the small ordinary things he does that you take for granted, the things that are important but normal and overlooked?

3 What are the things he likes about himself? How could you support the things he's proud of?

the other hand focus on the relationship dynamic and seem to be more affected by how they are treated, reacting to being ignored or taken for granted. But many women are also often unable to use even so-called constructive criticism well.

Diane, a sixty-one-year-old woman, brought Roland, her third husband, to their first session with me. She wanted me to help convince him that he was the cause of the problems in their relationship. As a professional therapist, I try to limit negativity because I know that ultimately this kind of session will have no positive benefit and will usually make things worse. Diane, however, was having none of this.

"I don't think you are hearing me." She raises her voice to make her point. "He does nothing for our relationship. If we go somewhere I have to plan it. He is indifferent to me, how I look, what I wear! I'm an attractive woman, but it doesn't seem to matter. He's so passive! He's driving me crazy! He doesn't even have an opinion about anything. I don't think I can live like this. This isn't the man I married. I'm sorry!"

Roland described himself as a retired CPA who still does some part-time work. Roland was widowed and spent ten years alone before marrying Diane, his second wife. When I asked Roland what problems he saw in Diane or the relationship the only one he could identify is that she is critical of him. "I love Diane. She's beautiful and a great cook. I've learned a lot from her about health and fitness. She's good to my children and grandchildren. I just wish she wouldn't complain about me so much."

 What if I don't like my boyfriend growing a beard and a ponytail and getting a big old tattoo. Do I just accept that this is him and be okay with it?—*Melody*

DEAR MELODY: Be interested in what this new look means for him. If you make it all about you, you won't *get* him— you'll get conflict instead.

I attempted to get Roland to verbalize the effect her criticism had on him, but he deflected my questions. I surmised that he might be afraid of exacerbating her anger by saying more. Frequently, people trapped in an environment where they feel put down will adopt a passive-aggressive stance. Believing that the expectations of them are impossible, they give up trying, or subtly get back at the criticizer by becoming passive or deliberately messing up, and then innocently denying that it was intentional.

"I want Diane to be happy," Roland says looking out the window. Paradoxically, men whose partners are unhappy and depressed often don't want to dwell on their inability to fix the problem and instead turn away from the relationship, getting involved in other things that are more satisfying. Women frequently don't understand why when they complain and need something their man is absorbed in TV, playing golf, or working longer hours, as was the case with Roland who probably felt inadequate and was retreating as a common defensive maneuver.

Recognize the Positives

If criticizing yourself or others does not motivate positive change, what will produce more desirable behavior? Research points to newer workplace strategies that emphasize a worker's strengths, contributions, and qualities that make a difference in production. Inspired employers even use work-life balance and support systems like childcare and onsite laundries to maximize their employees' time and engender good feelings and attitudes.

If you adapt this idea to your relationship, you'll see that recognizing your partner's contribution and strengths will make him feel good and may cause him to want to do more, but you don't want to be positive solely to manipulate your partner into changing. However, if you notice the small things your partner does and praise him for his efforts it may encourage that behavior, but you do these things without expecting or needing it to result in something you want. This is an important piece. By giving up the notion that you know what's right for your partner, you can be positive and complimentary without manipulation. Ask for what you want, but don't be attached to a particular outcome.

Strengthen the Connection

Diane came back the following week without Roland. She confessed that she was put off by my insistence that she was responsible for at least 50 percent of the problem, but was intrigued by my approach and willing to look at herself since other marriage counseling hadn't worked. Here is what I told her: Acceptance is the highest relationship ideal. It is the essence of positive relating.

Unreserved acceptance is, in our deepest place, what we want from ourselves and each other. As I helped Diane realize that she could make beginning attempts to move in this direction, I'd like to show you how you might come to this more peaceful place.

Increase Acceptance

Begin by taking that issue that drives you nuts, that flaw in your man that rubs you raw, the almost daily irritation or hurt, and look at the meaning you give to it—figure out why it is such a big deal for you. Underneath these criticisms there is a need that is not being met, a desire that is being thwarted.

Diane defended her need at first, "Hey, what's so wrong about wanting someone to take an interest in the life you share together, participate, have some ideas, some feelings, something to contribute, initiate something, even state an opinion!" She believed I didn't understand her dilemma, but I understood it all too well. There arc few women who experience the depth and quality of connection that they dream of having. Most, like Diane, see their situation as below normal.

I encouraged Diane to go further and help me understand the importance Roland's interest had for her. "I think it means love to me. Yes, I can hear that Roland loves me but it's wanting to be with me and enjoy me that really says love." When I probed about Diane's childhood, she focused on an abusive alcoholic father who eventually abandoned the family. She was involved with boys early and craved male attention. Diane felt like a failure; this was her third marriage and she was still struggling with these issues.

Consider the Meaning of Behaviors

The meaning that women give their partners' traits or behaviors is often incorrect. There are numerous reasons that people act or respond the way they do. It may be useful to understand a partner's motivation, but sometimes that isn't forthcoming, or is a complex combination of things. You may overlook what might be there because you deem it to be insignificant or "not enough."

In couples' counseling with a previous therapist, Roland said that by giving Diane a lot of control over their life together he was ensuring that they would have the lifestyle most pleasing to her; he wanted her to be happy. I saw this as a bit simplistic and believed more was at stake for him. It's likely he wants to avoid conflict and stifles his own ideas and opinions to avoid negativity, which no doubt creates even more negativity. What I told Diane is that in the bigger picture Roland's behavior doesn't actually matter. Her job is to make it alright that he does what he does.

Never Tolerate Disrespect

I told Diane that every time she felt those familiar feelings of anger, irritation, or resentment that it was an opportunity for her to say to herself, *it's okay for him to be this way. It doesn't mean anything. I can accept this and practice letting it go.* I suggested that she practice the mantra *let him be as he is* but she needed more of an explanation. She had the erroneous belief that she was letting him off the hook, giving him a free pass. Diane was like a lot of women who think that if they accept their partner they will become a doormat and allow themselves to be mistreated or abused.

That is certainly not what I'm advocating. There is an important difference in your response to a partner who is speaking to you disrespectfully or treating you in a demeaning way. It is always necessary to flag such an occurrence and say directly and simply, *I do not like how you're speaking to me, or how you're treating me. Please stop.* In those situations it makes sense to disengage from him until later when you both can talk about it rationally.

This is very different from accepting treatment and behavior that you simply don't like.

I explained to Diane that by accepting Roland as he is, she lets herself off the hook. She isn't attached to his behavior, letting her buttons be pushed, or—most important—re-wounding herself. I pointed out to her that, by expecting Roland to do what he isn't willing or able to do, she recreates the same kind of situation she had with her father.

Diane understood the connection. "What I think you're telling me is that I'm letting Roland hurt me like my dad did. My dad wasn't the dad I wanted and needed. I'm creating the same situation with Roland." She finally understood that while she can't control what Roland says or does, she does have control over how his traits and behaviors affect her.

Let the Positives Shine

When you can eliminate your negative reactions or at least neutralize them, the positive qualities of your man will be much more apparent. It's helpful to look at where you partner came from, the things that shaped his childhood, the obstacles he had to overcome, and the strength of character that attracted you when you were first together.

See the Big Picture

Diane shifted her view of Roland to see how happy he was to support her ideas and get involved in whatever was important to her. When she planned a family get-together, he was eager to help with the food, barbeque the meat, play endless games of croquet or badminton with the grandkids, take pictures and get them downloaded for the slideshow on the TV, and help with cleanup

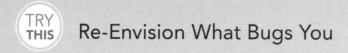

TRY THIS

Re-Envision What Bugs You

1   What is the primary thing that you keep trying to change in your man? Which trait is hardest to accept?

2   Consider how life would be if you made it okay for him to be this way, stopped personalizing his behavior as something hurtful to you, and just learned to live with him as he is.

3   How might you shift your view of him to a bigger picture? Can you see his perceived flaws in the context of his whole personality, and not just fixate on what's wrong?

until the last load of dishes was done. She saw him managing their money and securing their retirement with his investment strategies, staying in touch with his children and grandchildren even though she disparaged his monetary gifts to them when she would have preferred personal things. What she had at first liked about him in the beginning of their relationship—that he was easygoing and accommodating and fit in well with her friends and family—she began to be more positive about now which began to neutralize her negative view of him.

One of the most amazing insights Diane brought in to the last session we had together was her new understanding of the fact that she had a strong personality with definite opinions and that she had helped shape Roland's passivity by rejecting and disparaging his ideas in deference to her own. If she asked what he wanted for dinner and he said steak, she'd say they ate too much beef. If he suggested they go to the outdoor music theater, she'd complain that it was too hot. She began to see how she nipped his ideas, how she contributed to his passivity, and realized that he was sensitive and reactive to her responses. "As I've relaxed my pressure on him, surprisingly he risks a tad more. He'll comment on my outfit or praise the dinner I've cooked. He had an idea yesterday to invite the neighbors over for cards. I'm not a great card player like he is, but I thought it would be good to go along with him and it was fun. Before I may have nixed the idea."

 How can I give my guy positive feedback if he doesn't do a darn thing?—*Kathryn*

DEAR KATHRYN: See if your anger and high expectations are getting in the way of appreciating ordinary things like the fact that he goes to work, gets the mail, picks up some milk, or engages you in a nice conversation.

Use Both Right- and Left-Brain Functions

Notice that here is another example of how left-brain activities are focused on narrow vision, seeing only one part of a situation, whereas right brain awareness is inclusive, seeing the big picture and taking in the whole. The left brain, when active in women, focuses on analysis, judgment, criticism, and being correct, whereas when the right brain is activated they are able to see connection, similarities, and find confluence. Of course everyone has both functions, but it may take practice over time to see the beauty, recognize the positives, and enjoy the okay-ness of your larger life instead of getting stuck on small differences and correcting one problem after another.

Thoughts Attract More of the Same

The law of attraction—the belief that the kind of energy you create attracts the same kind of energy in return—is a metaphysical concept that has gotten a lot of attention recently, although it's not a new idea. Whatever thoughts you hold create an energy pattern that manifests into a reality. Our thoughts create our feelings and mood and that affects our behavior. This is actually the basis for a highly researched and effective form of therapy—cognitive therapy, which I described in Chapter 3.

When you apply the law of attraction to your partner and your relationship, you can see that when you hold negative ideas about him you focus on these examples and the negativity expands. Because women are so oriented toward relationships, you may personalize and give meaning to things your partner does that cast it in a negative light when he may not have that intention. For example, you may be upset when your man chooses another activity over being with you, when he doesn't dress up to please you, when he is distracted and not paying attention to your story, or when he forgets to do what you ask him to do. To a woman these may be things that *prove* he doesn't care about her. Your man may complain that you are too sensitive and too easily hurt since these things wouldn't affect him. Accepting that many occurrences in your life as a couple do not have the meaning that you assign to them and that you may in fact personalize a lot of neutral events can help reduce conflict.

Consider **YOUR** Mindset   It's paradoxical, but when you get out of the way with your own needs and ideas of how your man should be, you can see more clearly how he is and develop more respect for his qualities and character traits—even returning to the appreciation you had for him at the beginning of your relationship. Surprisingly, your man—or your view of him—may change when you stop the tugging and manipulation, and there is often a shift in the way you are together. Acceptance is a phenomenal tool, both for yourself and for him. You learn not only to be okay with him and things as they are, but you also give up the notion that you have the power or the responsibility to create him or the relationship into a thing of splendor. You realize that being attached and driven to have things a certain way is only a recipe for conflict and suffering.

 Share YOUR Views

Discuss this chapter in your book club or women's circle, or with friends:

1 How have you been portrayed by your parents or teachers in a way that didn't serve you well? Were there traits you overcame or outgrew that continue to be reinforced?

2 It's hard for some women to give up their dream image or fantasy man and accept that their spouse is never going to be that person. Does that tendency create disharmony and problems for you? Is it possible that you're not meeting his fantasy expectations either?

3 Why is it difficult to stop criticizing and nagging even when you see the outcome of these behaviors? What is the effect on you when your man doesn't see your point or want your input, and resists the things you believe are in his best interest?

CHAPTER 7

TOGETHER— POLISHED NOT PERFECT

In your desire to be loved, appreciated, and valued you may do things that actually keep you from getting what you want. Sacrificing yourself to please your partner, playing a subordinate role in the relationship, and pretending to be someone you aren't can have a deleterious effect on your happiness and will ultimately affect your man and your relationship. A man is inexplicably drawn to a happy woman, is recharged by her radiant energy, but conversely defends himself against her rainstorm of negativity and complaints. It's likely that if you dispense love as a reward and are only giving to get in the relationship, you may create anger and resentment for both of you.

Men and women do not share relationship skills and interests equally, and more of the responsibility for creating a positive connection may fall to you. When you have the courage to seek your own approval and ask for what you want, you'll magnetize the respect and love you crave without the need to earn it. Feeling good about yourself allows you to be naturally open and receptive.

We Teach Others How to Treat Us

If you ponder this idea carefully, you may realize that it is a powerful truth that is filled with astonishing possibilities for you and your man: *When you love yourself, your amazing body, and your life, and delight in your incredible existence, you'll be a radiant woman, and your man will bask in your light and reflect your glow.* Nothing increases your man's mood, productivity, and pleasure like your being a happy, fulfilled woman. He'll often take credit for your happiness because pleasing you is so important to him, but he won't be as open to taking responsibility for your negative states, which is why I've tried so hard to convince you to stop blaming and complaining.

 I am a big people pleaser. How do I start being more focused on my own needs?—*Carly*

> DEAR CARLY: Several times each day, ask yourself: *Is this in my best interest? Is this what I want? Does this meet my needs?* At first, you may feel uncomfortable when you aren't earning love, but eventually you'll like the new healthier you.

What does work is for you to become the leading lady, the heroine persona that you truly are and treat yourself the way you would want to be treated by your partner. Perhaps you've noticed that people intuitively pick up on the way you treat yourself and treat you similarly. If you put yourself down and point out your faults, others will criticize and poke malicious fun at you. If you expect to be the one who always does the cleanup and is the worker in the group, others will only be too happy to let you do it. If you routinely put others first and take the last seat and the crumbs, expect others to see this as you. Women often mistakenly think that others will reciprocate and give back in kind.

This rarely happens. Instead, others will probably continue to expect that you'll be the giver and they'll be the recipient. You inadvertently lead them to believe in your generosity of spirit and they like it that way.

Star in Your Own Production

To be a true heroine in your own life, you need to stop being what other people want you to be and be yourself. You'll have to stop taking all of these bit parts and star in your own production. This can be a very difficult thing for a woman to do and it may be scary to risk stepping out in this bold way. Because you have a female brain that is attuned to what others want and need, you may erroneously think that love is something you earn by pleasing others—and that your man gets your love by pleasing you. To style yourself as a man pleaser you may deny some aspects of yourself and play a personality that may not be authentic, which is maddening if you aren't rewarded for your efforts. This type of relating can be heavily conflicted since you're basically sacrificing yourself to be more of what your partner wants, and are tugging at him to meet more of your needs. To change this, it's necessary to make space in your relationship for both you and your partner to be as you are and evolve as your larger life directs.

Pleasing Yourself Pleases Him

Be prepared that others may not like your heroine personality and complain that you are not the same. This is not necessarily true for your man who may become interested in this new version of you even if you aren't always available to do his laundry or cook for him. When you're more interested in your needs and value yourself more he may see you in the same light and be more interested in pleasing you. You will be less like a mother, complaining and pointing out his problems, and more like an exciting woman who knows how to please herself.

You may even ask him to do things for you: rub your neck, bring you a cup of coffee or glass of wine, or suggest he make something to eat or get takeout. Men, because of their competitive natures, want to work for a prize. They devalue things that come too easily to them; if they require so little effort, they aren't worth having. Men want the highly desirable women that other men want and when you value yourself more, he may see you in the same way.

Your happier, less needy heroine persona will also reflect positively on him and he may feel more energy and excitement himself because of what you are radiating. This may manifest in greater sexual interest on his part, and sex is a perfect place to subtly shift the focus to you and your pleasure. By shaping your sexual encounters—not with words, but with sounds and hand gestures—you'll teach him how to give you a better experience, which is what he actually wants whether he knows it or not.

This reflected glow emanating from you may increase his mood and vitality because that is the nature of the masculine, to be attracted to the sun. When you were a storm cloud he probably needed to get away from you to keep his energy. Now that you are radiating light he may become more interesting, creative, and productive. Allowing him to have space, autonomy, and the support of your vibrant energy will encourage his greater purpose in the world, which will naturally fulfill him because men are normally fixated on making a contribution in this way. Then, because he is satisfied and expanded in this purposeful existence, he will be even more content and pleased with you. Of course it may take some time for you to shift into your heroine persona and learn to love and enjoy yourself whether he is initially supportive or not.

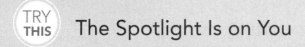

The Spotlight Is on You

1   Just for a day put on your imaginary heroine costume and consider that your life is the only one you would want to live and that everything that happens is perfect for you to either enjoy or learn from. Believe that you're beautiful just the way you are and that you're totally loved. Look at yourself in the mirror and tell yourself that you're gorgeous. Recapture that feeling of being in love and hold it in your heart. Know you are special but not because a man says so.

2   For this one day, carry out your duties and respond to everyone as if you were a happy, satisfied woman, secretly loved, and radiating beauty. Allow that everything is okay as it is and resist nothing.

3   Look back at the end of the day and see if or how your thoughts and beliefs affected your mood and the reactions of others. What did you realize from doing this exercise?

4   Identify all the small ways that you could make yourself happier. Are there foods that would please you? Some time to yourself to pursue something that matters to you? An update of your makeup or hair? Building exercise into your day, spending more time with friends, or fewer chores?

5   How could you give yourself more of what you want? What standards could you reduce, shortcuts could you take, things you could eliminate? How could you take back some time and do more for yourself? What people would you want to see less often? What activities are not essential?

Love Is Not a Reward

Many women received conditional love—a type of approval—in childhood. When you were cooperative and obedient you received affection and warmth and when you were obstinate and problematic you were given the icy cold treatment. Don't continue this practice in your relationship. Instead, love your partner for who he is, the same way you want to be loved for who you are. You may not always like or approve of what your partner says or does, but stay present and loving and work things out. Love, or the withdrawal of love, is not a reward or a weapon. Love is a way to maintain your closeness even when you don't agree.

When you are in your man-pleasing mode to earn love, you may resist being open and honest and saying what you feel because it detracts from the image you're projecting. Stop all that and just say what you feel and want, but do it in such a way that it isn't a criticism or an attack on your man. Take the risk of being yourself and stop pretending to keep it safe or to manipulate him to be how you want. Opening up this way may make you feel more vulnerable since you won't be hiding. However, as you practice revealing yourself openly, speaking your truth will eventually become more comfortable for you. When you are fully grounded in your authentic heroine self you can be open and expressive without artifice and accepting and receptive without judgment. A woman's natural state is to be undefended when she feels good about herself.

Communicate Correctly

Request the things that you want from your man in simple, direct language without overtones of anger or resentment. For example, say: *I would enjoy watching this program with you so we could* discuss it afterward. *Would you clean up the dishes in the sink? Let's go to bed early and cuddle. I'd like you to wear something different to the party.* Express your feelings with statements that show you taking responsibility for your feelings and not blaming your man for them. For example, say: *When I don't get a chance to share my day with you I don't feel as close. When I clean up the house and it's a mess the next day my motivation to do it again is shot.* Without a righteous stance and making him wrong express your needs clearly and simply: *I feel special when you stop with the computer and hug me when I come home. This is a new outfit; what do you think of it? Would you think up something fun for us to do this weekend?*

Don't misconstrue this approach as magic. It will not right everything and will have success and failure. It will work sometimes and not other times. You need do this without expectation. Don't require the outcome to be what you envision. You'll then be able to accept whatever transpires and move on for your own growth and maturity. You'll experience freedom and groundedness no matter what happens. Try it. You may be surprised.

 What is the trick to asking for what I want? All I get back from my man is grumbling and dirty looks.—*Vickie*

DEAR VICKIE: Begin with the words *honey, would you be willing to* and then make your request. Make sure that it isn't a demand in disguise and accept his refusal as graciously as his assent.

Work It Out

Corinne, thirty-five, and Will, thirty-two, married after knowing each other just eight months when Corinne became pregnant. Their relationship was burdened by a difficult pregnancy and

Corinne's depression after the birth of their healthy baby girl, Taylor. Corinne felt overwhelmed by setting up a household together, having a new baby, and returning to her job at the bank. She believed Will had changed and, even though he seemed ready and excited to assume marriage and parenthood, she saw him as unwilling to make the sacrifices necessary to maintain their busy lifestyle. Most of the childcare and household responsibilities fell to her, even though they both had full-time jobs. She felt exhausted and unavailable for the social and sexual relationship that Will wanted. He left her to meet his buddies at the bar after work or play tournament soccer on Saturdays. She ended up spending time with her mother and complaining about her errant husband and even spent the night at her parent's house after an argument with Will.

When they came together to their first appointment, Will saw the situation differently from Corinne. "I would help more but she finds something wrong with everything I do. She's so particular and cautious about Taylor that I've given up trying to feed or bathe her. I tried doing some of the housework, but the laundry wasn't sorted right and the vacuuming wasn't good enough and some of the dishes ended up in the wrong cupboard when I cleaned up the kitchen. Everything I did it seemed was wrong." Corinne admitted that she obsessed over details. She complained that Will deliberately tried to bungle chores and did things sloppily to convince her to do them herself. Will agreed that maybe he did stop trying to please her.

Corinne discovered that she expected Will to be sensitive, to know what was needed, and to pitch in without having to be asked. He took her complaining and negativity as a reflection on him. They both were angry and unhappy. I coached them to take turns using active listening techniques, expressing their feelings and saying what they needed without any comment or rebuttal by the other. The listener then reflected what each heard from the partner. It became easier to solve the problems. Will agreed to do his own laundry, hire someone to do the cleaning to Corinne's specifications, and help out in the kitchen and with the baby. Corinne agreed to be more accepting of Will's style of helping and to be available to do things as a couple. But the most important thing each learned was how to listen and understand the viewpoints of their spouse.

Arguing and making your man wrong for how he views a problem doesn't fix anything. It only keeps you locked in the "right and wrong" game, blaming, attacking, and withholding love. This solution works best when the couple works their issues out together, but I also have seen it work effectively when one partner, usually the woman, uses these skills herself. It's not perfect but it can work.

Women Are Natural Leaders

My clients often complain that I expect more of women than I do of men, but this is true only in the relationship department. In our culture, women are socialized to make relationships a high priority, they generally have more relationship skills than men, and they are usually the ones who are asking for change. Men may carry the ball in other areas—yard work, financial support, or other functions—but they typically aren't the ones coming to a therapist to complain about their spouse. Since women are the driving force in the relationship you also have a lot of the power necessary to change the relationship by doing something different on your own. Not liking the situation and demanding equal participation will rarely resolve the problem.

Learn How to Listen and Talk

1 When your man is expressing strong feelings about something, see if you can listen and reflect what he is saying without arguing or offering your view. Repeat what you hear him say and understand what he wants you to hear and know.

2 Wait a while after the first session, but ask your man to listen to you without offering solutions or advice. Say something like, *I would like you to listen to my feelings without saying anything. I don't need you to offer advice or try to fix anything, just hear me out.* If he tries to argue or give solutions, respond with *I know you want to help me and I appreciate that, but you could help me best by just listening for now.*

3 Ask your partner to help with a chore or other activity. If it doesn't work out successfully, don't blame or complain. Simply ask again without a tone of disapproval or resentment.

4   Ask your partner when would be a good time to for you to discuss something with him. Express your feelings honestly and openly without blaming or making him wrong. Say something like *I'm feeling sad/left out/lonely/upset/angry/ troubled, and I would like to tell you about it. I started to believe _____ when you did _____ and this made me feel _____. I need some connection/reassurance/love/comfort/ or understanding from you.*

5   The next time you and your partner have a disagreement, see if you can continue to exude warmth, affection, and love even though you have conflict. Say something like, *I know we aren't seeing eye-to-eye about this but I want to still be close with you. Can we hug and still love each other while we're working this out?*

Help Him to Be More Relational

As a woman with more relationship needs and abilities, the work of the relationship may fall to you. You'll need to remind him of the things that matter to you, the special songs, memories, dates, or places that have meaning for your relationship. Sometimes women discount the things their man does if he didn't come up with the idea. For example, Corinne complains, "If I have to remind him to do something nice for me on Mother's Day, then what's the point?" The reality is that men are less equipped than women for relationships. It may not be something that is socialized into their make-up.

Men report that they have to write lists and reminders to do the things their mates appreciate, like a sentimental card or a surprise note in their lunch box. Since men may not enjoy those things themselves, they may not think of them on their own. However, typically, a man would be eager to please his woman if he only knew what to do. Because women can be such a mystery to men and pleasing them may seem like such a daunting task, it is a wise woman who provides her man with help in this regard. For example, one client of mine posted a wish list on the refrigerator with pictures, coupons, and ads. Men welcome appreciation for the things they do like servicing your car, or fixing things in the home, or making the money to keep your life going. While women don't necessarily consider these relationship activities, men do. While a woman may put more credence on spontaneous affection than a hot cup of coffee in the morning, to a man the coffee may speak of his love and connection just as much.

Focus on the Positives

Sex was an issue that Corinne had a conflict about. She was conscious of the fact that Will was always softened and opened by

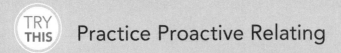

1   How could you help your partner be more relational?

2   What are the things you know he would be happy to do if you asked him?

3   What caring behaviors does he exhibit that you recognize or could see as loving?

4   How could you take responsibility for creating those good times that you and he enjoy?

their lovemaking and, for several days afterward, was responsive and attentive, doing the things that pleased her. When I asked her why she was then not more available for sex when she enjoyed it as well, her response was typical of many women "Am I not just using my body to get what I want? Shouldn't he be just as attentive and loving whether I have sex with him or not?" Corinne expressed her feelings well. She didn't want to feel like she was manipulating Will and just having sex to create harmony and connection. She wanted the harmony and connection to be there independently of sex. She believed that the connection resulting from sex was not as highly prized as the connection in their daily life together. Here is an example of how she gave meaning to something and then allowed it to influence what she felt and did. Many men tell me that the most connection they feel with their partner is during sex. It is the easiest way for them to feel

Enhance Attraction

1 How do you look, dress, or behave that your partner finds attractive and brings out his warmth and interest for you?

2 What do you do that your partner most appreciates and brags about? What makes him proudest of you?

3 When is your mate more open and receptive to your love and your feelings?

their intense feelings of love and attachment. Women's emotional bonding is also strengthened by a partner who desires and wants to enjoy and pleasure them. There is a truism that goes like this: Men need to make love to feel love; women need to feel loved to make love.

Wear Gratitude Glasses

In our quest for perfection, women often focus too much on what's wrong, analyzing and comparing, and miss the things that are wonderful. Gratitude is something that can shift our gears from what's wrong to what's right. Begin today to emphasize the gifts that your partner brings to your life. It might sound a bit morose, but try to think about how your life would be changed if he were no longer here, what you would miss, and the ways he contributes to your happiness and well-being that would be

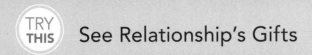

See Relationship's Gifts

1 How has your partner affected you positively?

2 What have you learned by being in this relationship?

3 What qualities does your partner recognize and reinforce in you?

4 How do you feel when you're with your partner in a social setting?

5 How have you changed and grown in this relationship?

gone. The best gift you can give your man is to be happy with him and your life together. When you're happy, his tendency will be to move toward your satisfied positive nature and add to your happiness.

Forgive the Past

As is frequently the case, you may have a backlog of resentments and problems that occurred years ago that you're still holding onto. They may be breaches of trust, lapses of judgment, or

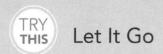

Let It Go

1 Could you consider that when your partner did hurtful things he had a lapse of judgment and didn't intend to harm you?

2 In the past, have you had expectations of your partner that were not possible for him to easily satisfy?

3 Has your partner grown in ways that make it unlikely that he will repeat the hurtful things he may have done in the past?

4 How would you benefit by erasing your memory of those events?

things that were genuinely hurtful and created a huge rift in the relationship. How do you let those things go? Where does the necessary forgiveness come from? First you need to see what holding onto those memories and resentments does for you.

 It's scary to go off and do things that please me. Won't my boyfriend decide to do things on his own too and ruin our relationship?—*Emma*

DEAR EMMA: A tight hold can strangle a relationship, increase expectations, and generate conflict and resentment. Be brave, work on your anxiety, and create some space for both of you to grow.

Some clients tell me that they believe if they allow their man to forget what he did, he may do something like that again. For example, if you don't remind him from time to time about coming onto your best friend that night he was drunk, or bring up the year he completely forgot your anniversary, he may do those things again. The constant reminders are a kind of insurance to keep your man from hurting you again. Other women use old issues to make their partners look like bozos or fools. Then you don't expect anything more, and if he does hurtful things you can write it off. Others may hold onto past resentments and old hurts because they want to build a defense system and to protect themselves by being prepared in case it happens again. No matter the reason, holding onto old hurts and continuing to dwell on them will only wound you. Letting go of things that are over, can't be changed, and are no longer happening is for your benefit.

Consider YOUR Mindset   I hope you're seeing that the purpose of a relationship is not for someone else to give you what you need to make you happy. It isn't necessary to hide or distort your authentic self to be pleasing to your man and get love. It is much more likely that, as you expand into your biggest heroine persona and take the risk to make yourself happy and fulfilled, that your partner will be even more attracted to you. There is power for a woman in being open with her feelings and needs. It reflects an acceptance of yourself and who you are and is really the badge of inner beauty. By giving up your conditional love, for love that is genuine, you and your partner will stay close despite your differences, and will be able to express your needs and feelings without rancor and bitterness. Respecting each other and your different views of the world will only enhance your relationship—not hurt it. Being more honest will take courage on your part, but you'll benefit by doing so. Being fully yourself and accepting your man can affect your entire relationship dynamic.

Discuss this chapter in your book club or women's circle, or with friends:

1 How has your man responded to your moods? Does it seem that he is more interested in you when you're happy and less so when you are down?

2 Manipulating men is a time-honored practice that most women have used to get what they want. What do you see as the upside or downside to this practice?

3 Why is it hard for women to do what most men do naturally—put themselves first in their lives? How was your growing up experience different from the way boys were socialized?

CHAPTER 8

RELATIONSHIP'S BIGGER PRIZE

Your relationship provides you with the best way to know yourself, to see the places where you need to change and grow, and to gain the maturity to manage the frustrations and conflicts that are a normal part of life. Too many women assume that their man is the problem in the relationship and getting him to change or moving on to another better model will correct the unhappiness they are experiencing. Those of you who bailed on a relationship only to see the same difficulty reappear in a slightly different version will understand that it's necessary to look within for some answers.

Frequently, what women originally see as a man's strength later becomes a source of annoyance, and what they're actually demanding from him is not a behavior change, but a complete personality transplant. By exploring other options for understanding and acceptance, you can create more peace for yourself and for your relationship. You can lead by example and demonstrate a non-defensive posture, honor your partner's limitations, and strengthen your own character in the process.

Consider Your Options

1   Is it possible for me to be okay with the situation and my
    partner if nothing changes?

2   Am I making more of this than I need to?

3   Do I have choices that I'm not seeing or exercising?

4   Are there deeper, unresolved issues of mine that I
    could explore?

5   What other solutions are there to this problem besides
    him changing?

The Relationship Tour

Okay, your desire for a relationship was self-serving. You wanted to be loved, cherished, adored, taken care of, appreciated, and valued. You wanted to be together with someone in bliss and ecstasy. You definitely didn't sign on for the lifelong frustration a committed relationship can bring. Living intimately with another person is like living in a house of mirrors. If you pay attention you have an amazing opportunity to learn so much about yourself—more even than seeing a therapist—and it's free. There can be repressed feelings and needs, old wounding, and resentments, not to mention almost daily button-pushing episodes. If you see these upsets and problems as proof of your partner's deficiencies, you will only be building your case to leave. In every area of your life, frustration has been your teacher—so why not now? You learned how to tie your shoes that way, how to master the intricacies of the computer, how to dance the tango, snowboard, or play tennis. Use your frustration to look at your relationship. What a revelation that can be for those brave enough to take a look especially if you're angry, upset, despairing, depressed, and waking up at night plotting revenge on your man. It can be humbling to take responsibility for your contribution to the problem and see where you need to change. Any time you're unable to resolve a problem using a simple request or an honest expression of feeling, you need to consider a different road.

Growth Opportunities Await You

Seeing the potential for growth that your partner presents for you is one of the greater purposes you can find in a frustrating or challenging relationship. All relationships have the potential of showing you where you need to change, and where you need to grow to find peace and contentment. Keep in mind that conflict is healthy and normal in a relationship. Couples who vow that they never disagree are among the unhealthiest as there is usually an undercurrent of repressed feelings and perhaps a pattern of roleplaying and inauthentic behavior. Welcoming conflict and seeing it as natural and necessary reduces the likelihood of making it a problem. Sometimes rethinking or detaching from a problem you were fixated on will give you a new perspective. Perhaps you can understand how your partner became the way he now is or how his childhood wounding factored into his current behavior.

 My partner is a slob and is okay with a messy apartment. I always have to do the housework because he doesn't care. What can I do?—*Tatiana*

DEAR TATIANA: Because of your high standards, he may have quit trying to please you. Notice his small efforts and give positive feedback. Do chores together and make them fun. If he's a keeper, relax your expectations.

This was the case for Abby and her husband Dan. She constantly bristled at his unwanted advice and repeated lecturing. He often tried to explain current events, how things worked, economics, and politics to her, to the point where she felt demeaned and put down. "He must think I'm an idiot!" She complained. However, if she had probed a little more deeply into Dan's early experiences, she'd see that Dan is the product of his critical demanding father. Underneath his self-possessed exterior is a little boy who is showing off what he knows, trying to convince people that he is good enough and smart enough. This idea surprised Abby. "You're right!" She said. "I can see how he isn't putting me down, but trying to build himself up by impressing me."

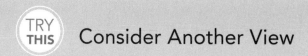

TRY THIS — Consider Another View

1. Identify the behaviors or personality traits you dislike about your partner and see them in the context of his childhood wounding. How is he compensating for how he was treated?

2. How could you view these traits in a neutral way, instead of as a statement about you?

3. What qualities does your relationship need from you? What are you being called upon to develop? Patience? Acceptance? Self-support?

She detached from Dan's annoying behavior and now doesn't take it personally. Learning to detach and not personalize your partner's behavior is a wonderful skill in intimate relationships.

There Are Reasons to Stay

Who hasn't thought about leaving a relationship? After a particularly difficult argument when unkind words are exchanged on both sides, the hurt and pain may make leaving seem like the only alternative. Abby was at that point when she first came to see me. She described Dan's lack of interest in her and his defensiveness when she tried to approach him, his style of parenting where he tried to be the playful fun dad with the two girls and left all the discipline to her, and their demanding jobs which left them functioning like roommates. For her the task of relating seemed impossible.

117

Abby described situations that made her so angry and frustrated that the only solution she could imagine was to separate from Dan.

I'm reluctant to support a client's leaving a relationship prematurely. I see numerous people who are dealing with the same or similar issues repeatedly with different partners and it seems obvious that the problem is not about finding someone new. Frequently, women return to therapy struggling with the same problems despite finding a new partner who, on the surface, looked vastly different from the last one.

Leaving May Be a Revolving Door

Two things happen when you leave a relationship without considering the growth opportunity it is offering you: (1) you will be attracted to similar men and will find someone with patterns and behaviors remarkably like the partner you just left, or (2) since you have not changed your own ideas and styles of relating you'll actually shape your new relationship to be like the familiar one you rejected.

The reality is that the relationship you have now offers you a wonderful opportunity to learn something. It is a mirror, reflecting what you most need to know about yourself. It is a workshop designed especially for you that will challenge and frustrate you and, in so doing, will create a perfect learning environment for your evolution. By running away and finding someone else, you only delay the learning. A new relationship may offer you the very same lesson.

Staying Can Make You Healthier

I'll give you the same advice I gave to Abby. Stay for now and use the problems in this situation to become a healthier person.

That in itself may make the relationship work, but in the event it doesn't, you'll be in a position to attract a healthier person the next time around. If you leave now, you will be back at this place again but sooner the next time.

 Threatening to leave always makes my husband kick in gear for a while. Without that how would I get him to show any interest in our marriage?—*Maggie*

DEAR MAGGIE: This is a lose-lose game you two are playing. Redirect this wasted energy and spice up your own life and mood. He will either sink further or choose to swim after you.

A useful technique is to stop using the fantasy of breaking up as an escape valve. Decide to not even consider that as an option for a set period of time—six months, or one year, for example—and close the door on the possibility of separation. This doesn't have to be a joint decision, although that is ideal. The purpose of this commitment is for you to throw yourself into the relationship wholeheartedly. It also requires you to focus on doing the work and making the changes you need to make without another option to consider. If you were in the habit of threatening divorce in the heat of arguments, it's a good idea to stop that practice even with yourself and function as though you are totally committed to your relationship.

Reconsider His Traits

Frequently, what women find so attractive initially later becomes a problem. If you were attracted to someone determined to be a business success and his work ethic and drive were attractive to

TRY THIS   Study His Character

1 What originally attracted you to your present mate?

2 Are you still attracted to these qualities or do you see them in a different light?

3 What things are you critical about in your partner?

4 Which of the things that you view as negative about your partner are also qualities you dislike in yourself?

you, are you complaining now that he is all work and no play and has no time for you? If you enjoyed your mate's constant devotion in the beginning, are you now feeling smothered by his obsessive attention? Were you attracted to your man's cockiness and self-confidence when you first met, but now re-label these qualities as narcissism and self-centeredness? The initial attraction connects with that childlike place in you that wants to make up for what was missing when you were growing up. Later on, you may want something else from the relationship and turn the strength into a flaw.

Abby was confused when I told her she needed to use her relationship to learn about herself. She asked, "But if he's the one with the problem, why am I the one to change?" This is a question I get frequently when a client is convinced that everything would be fine if her partner would change. I helped her see that what she called a problem was actually a strength in disguise, something she had liked or loved about him at an earlier point in their being together. Abby admitted that she was attracted to Dan's fun-loving nature when they first met. He was funny and fun to be with. They laughed a lot, which was new for her. Now it seems that fun-loving nature is the problem. "He acts like a kid and doesn't take responsibility. He doesn't want to discipline the girls and finds every excuse to play. I've become his mother!"

"I think Dan's playfulness is a real asset in your relationship," I explained to Abby. "Think for a moment what would happen if he was just like you." Abby agreed that she was the dutiful one, the one who had high standards for how the house looked, for paying bills the day they came in, for putting work—any kind of work—before fun. That's what she learned growing up. "Could you see how Dan's personality is a good thing, that he can be a kind of teacher, helping you to be less serious and showing you how to laugh more, play more?" I could tell Abby was softening to my line of reasoning; she was beginning to understand where this could go. "Not everything can be fixed or changed. Dan may never be much of a disciplinarian. He may not be comfortable in that role."

Change Behaviors, Not Personalities

It's hard to admit and accept that there will be things in your relationship that can't be corrected or changed. Both you and your partner have unique personalities and wide-ranging influences that have shaped your behavior over the years. Despite seeing the value in doing things a certain way, your partner will not be comfortable with every adaptation you may want him to make. To determine if your request is a reasonable one, consider whether it is a behavior change or a personality change that you want.

For example, Abby could ask Dan to take a turn at paying bills or take the kids to their soccer practice—a behavioral change, but requiring him to take notice, remember schedules, and see jobs that needed to be done, would be a personality change and difficult considering his nature. You can ask for the behavior you want from your partner, but you need to respect that he won't develop characteristics that cause him to think or act the way you do.

 I guess I don't really want to be a mature grown-up person in a relationship. My parents spoiled me rotten. How do I get my husband to keep spoiling me?—*Frankie*

DEAR FRANKIE: Seriously, princess types have it hard and you may have been wounded by so much indulgence. There is a lot you will miss by not growing up. Start now by looking to yourself instead of him for some of what you need.

It's easier to see a solution to a problem when the problem is not framed as a personality flaw. When Abby said she needed help with parenting and identified ways that Dan could provide this, it was easier to gain his cooperation. In the past, when she complained he was irresponsible, the problem couldn't be solved. Look at the way you are framing the problems in your relationship. Could it be that what you're seeing as a defect in your partner could be reworked as a simpler problem that has a solution? For example, instead of framing the problem by saying that your man is emotionally distant, change the problem to be the fact that your family needs to spend more time together. Instead of

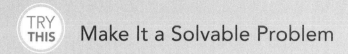

TRY THIS   Make It a Solvable Problem

1   Identify a negative personality trait in your man and see if
    you can reframe it as a solvable problem instead.

2   What behaviors could you ask your partner to provide
    without expecting him to initiate them?

3   What did you find attractive about your partner initially that
    you are having a problem with now? How could you see this
    as a strength, a balance to your personality, or a positive to
    your own growth?

labeling your man as secretive, could you change the problem to be the need for better communication?

React Non-Defensively

In Chapter 1, we discussed how complaints and criticisms are usually ineffective in creating change and can often backfire. You may have experienced this yourself: responding to attacks with counterattacks escalates verbal violence and exacerbates resentment and anger. It's useful to use a different strategy when you are the one being criticized. There is also the possibility that, as you lead by example, your partner will follow.

We can learn an important lesson by looking at martial arts. The martial arts approach is to skillfully take the oncoming force and redirect it to dismantle the attacker and diffuse the hit. It takes a certain amount of adaptability to redirect the energy rather than to fight back and oppose it directly. The philosophy underpinning this approach is to see that the hit provides an opportunity in disguise; every hit contains a positive or a blessing. To apply this theory to your relationships, be non-defensive when experiencing an attack of criticism and see if you can join with the energy of the attacker rather than opposing it.

If your man complains and pouts when you have plans separate from his, don't see it as an attack and defend yourself and your innocent plan to go shopping with a girlfriend. Instead, join with his energy. Interpret his complaint as a compliment and respond sweetly with appreciation that you know he'll miss you and wants to be with you. If he's waiting to go somewhere and complaining about your obsessive kitchen sanitation, cheerfully suggest that he can help you disinfect the counters. If he's nagging you about your resistance to sex, tell him about a role-playing game you read about which begins with him putting the kids to bed, making you a drink, and massaging your neck. You get the picture. Keep in mind that I would never suggest tolerating demeaning or disrespectful behavior from your man. If that occurs, it is necessary to flag it immediately and refuse to engage with him if he is treating you that way.

What Do You Expect of Him

Could it be that you talk too much, have too much to share with your partner, or expect him to be available to hear long, involved explanations and stories? If he's distracted, doesn't respond, or isn't listening, do you feel hurt, rejected, and devalued? Instead of crowding or overwhelming your man with long, detailed monologues about your day, give a few cliffhangers and wait to see if he bites. Don't use this approach as a test, to see if he cares, or to make him wrong if he doesn't want to hear more. It's for you to value yourself and your experiences and to wait until there's receptivity from him before you share them.

Men usually have difficulty with receptivity and are quick to offer solutions, or a rebuttal. So when you say *you'll never guess who I ran into today*, or *I found the best bargain*, or *Mary Jo called with news today*, pause and wait. If he has that glazed over look in his eyes or that blank stare like he doesn't know what his line should be, just let it go. Try again later. You could prattle on about everything that happened since you parted that morning but why? He is not receptive. It is not wrong for him to be disengaged, it's just the way he is.

You might be saying, *but he's never receptive.* Try reducing the number of times you expect him to listen to you and see if he isn't naturally drawn to dialogue. Men tell me they often feel overwhelmed by the amount of emotionally laden talk their woman wants them to hear and respond to. When you reduce your monologues, he may naturally move into the void you create and want to know about you and your day.

You could also describe what you need from him and say something like, *sharing about our time apart is how I like to connect with you* and see if that makes it possible for him to be more responsive. If not, practice being accepting of that and find other outlets to share your feelings and experiences. *But I want him to be interested in me. I want to share my day with him!* you wail. I hear you. That is ideal but not something you can demand. It's like grace, satisfying and beautiful if it happens, but not something you are entitled to.

Keep It Positive

1   How could you join with your man's energy, agree with what he is saying, or see a positive element to what seemed at first to be a negative?

2   Do you have a conflict that could be resolved by redirecting the energy rather than opposing it?

3   Is there a situation where you could resist defending yourself or your position, stay open, and consider another viewpoint and see what part of it you could accept?

4   In a situation where you can't agree, say *I can understand how you feel that way or came to that conclusion.* You can hear and understand his position without agreement.

Consider YOUR Mindset It's liberating to see that you can be alright even if your partner does not change in the ways that you at first found necessary. To fully accept someone takes understanding of why or how they formed in this particular way. It may require you to give up a little or a lot of what you thought was critically important or absolutely necessary to be happy. It may necessitate that you rearrange your ideas about life and function in a way that compensates for what you are not able to get from your partner. Acceptance is the greatest gift you can give any relationship. It is a way of being with another person that doesn't make demands on them, attempt to shape them, or pressure them to fulfill your expectations. Amazingly, when you can offer a person such unconditional acceptance, which in its purest form is the highest kind of love, they are apt to want to please and pleasure you, although you shouldn't use this as a manipulative device.

Allowing your partner to be as he chooses is the highest calling in an intimate relationship. When you give your partner this acceptance you simultaneously extend that same blessing to yourself. You learn self-acceptance along with acceptance of others. You can still be aware of your man's faults, problems, or flaws, and wish that he was different, but you are accepting what is for now, making what you have now right and good. This has a powerful effect on both yourself and your partner. You are able to see the value in being together, doing your work to evolve as an accepting mature person, and recognizing the grace flowing into your life.

Discuss this chapter in your book club or women's circle, or with friends:

1 Many women find it hard to accept that men are not able to provide the emotional support they want. What strategies have you used to strengthen your man's ability to focus on emotional issues and be more available?

2 How do your relationships encourage you to grow and mature? What experiences have you had that demonstrate where you came from and where you are now?

3 Men typically use anger as a multipurpose tool. How have you been able to respond positively to his complaints or anger and resist the urge to return the negativity with more of the same?

CHAPTER 9

EMPATHY—MAKE THE CONNECTION

One of the biggest gifts you can give your relationship is empathy. Learning how to use empathic responses and seeing both your partner and yourself as having a unique version of truth or reality is a powerful tool in resolving conflicts amicably and defusing arguments that will have no good outcome. There is nothing that conveys love—or deepens your understanding of your partner—more than experiencing life through his eyes, feelings, and viewpoints.

To understand empathy and use it selectively, a woman must first clean up the messes she has made with her open heart and caring nature. Growing up in a chaotic, dysfunctional household where picking up cues was a protective device may have heightened your normal sensitivity to other's moods and feelings. You may now feel drained and overwhelmed with everyone else's problems or be chronically victimized by everyone needing and using you. If this sounds like you, it's essential that you take on the task of boundary-setting, limit the non-reciprocating people in your life, and protect your time and energy so you can be totally present and available when it truly matters.

Empathy is easy to learn but difficult to implement because women naturally want to counter with their own opinions and override ideas that are considered stupid or wrong. The ability to listen with your whole being is extremely powerful in making profound connections and diffusing conflict. Especially with a man who may not have been supported emotionally as a child, empathy can open up his feelings and soften him in an amazing way. You may be unaware of the value in offering the gift of empathy to a man when he is unable or unwilling to return it, but you'll find that there are enormous benefits to both you and your relationship regardless of whether your partner follows your lead or not.

Sensitivity Requires Limits

Whether from biology or socialization, many women are blessed with sensibilities that may not always feel like a gift. Maybe you were like I was as a child, and your highly sensitive nature— especially if your environment was stressful and problematic— made you attuned to the subtleties and nuances of everyone and everything. Sometimes it was not possible to detect where your own feelings left off and your awareness of another began. If you were powerless to manage the painful realities of your young life, it may have become necessary to armor and desensitize yourself just to function.

If you are a sensitive adult, you need to understand that most of the data constantly pouring in no longer require your response. Maybe as a child you needed to pay attention to all the crazy stuff that would blindside you or create chaos. But now as you align with your grounded true self, you need to discard information that is not your business, such as others' moods, feelings, negativity, judgments, acting-out behaviors, and other problems that have nothing to do with you. This will demand a different kind

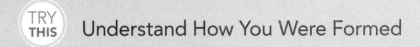

TRY
THIS

Understand How You Were Formed

1 Were you super-sensitive as a child?

2 Was your environment one that required you to pay attention to shifting moods and problems brewing?

3 What situations caused you stress because of your sensitivity, wanting acceptance and love, or the need to be safe?

4 How might you have desensitized yourself, through alcohol, drugs, or psychic armor to keep from feeling too much?

of vigilance at first as you practice noticing the data as a brief blip on your radar screen before you let them go. In the past this information may have been personalized and reacted to resulting in energy drains and emotional exhaustion, but now you can put up your deflector shields and stay snug and relaxed.

Decide What's Important

How do you tell if someone's feelings or behaviors should concern you? Well, if you have a relationship with the person there may be a reason to consider the data. Otherwise, why worry if people you don't know or have little connection with are angry, moody, acting out, or expressing negativity? People who lack boundaries in the most extreme form are those with road rage who personalize and react to neutral events that occur all the time. There is even wisdom in not reading the moods of and reacting to people you know and care about. It's better to assume that, as functional, mature adults, they'll take care of their own needs and ask for help if they want it.

 I feel guilty if I say no to people who are always asking me to do things. Then my boyfriend complains I'm exhausted when he wants to spend time together. What should I do?—*Susan*

DEAR SUSAN: Guilt is what keeps you stuck in old patterns. You must tolerate the bad feelings that are common when you try new healthy behaviors and support yourself until they become more natural.

Trickier to deal with are the needy people who you may have coached into depending on your advice, support, and comfort. I had a collection of people like this that I actually thought were friends. These are not reciprocal two-way relationships; these people exploit your kind heart and good nature and see your generosity as a one-way street. They take too much and give back too little. You will need to set boundaries here and limit the energy drain.

Be prepared for guilt to rear its head when you try new behaviors. This isn't the healthy guilt that gives you useful information when what you're doing is wrong, but the neurotic kind that keeps you stuck in old patterns. It will require a lot of self-support to push on through those voices that try to scare you into giving in, but you can't form a new healthy character if you continue to act in the old familiar ways. It will take some courage to be able to hang out in the new place until you feel more comfortable there.

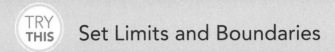

TRY THIS   Set Limits and Boundaries

1. What people exploit your good nature and expect more from you than they give? How can you limit the time and attention they require from you?

2. What positives do you get from these exchanges? Why do you think you encourage these dependent people?

3. How can you make the changes that will discourage these types of friendships?

4. What is at risk if you cultivate more two-way friendships and stop the excessive giving?

Plug the Energy Drain

It is a delusion that your energy is inexhaustible. Energy is just like money and must be managed that way. To make energy you need to do fun and fulfilling things, be with re-energizing people, relax in nature, or regroup in a solitary retreat. Energy is precious, and when you are being drained, you must put a stop to it. This may make you feel awful, but you need to support yourself and say: *I may feel mean and guilty, but those feelings are old and do not accurately reflect my current experience. I am acting in my own healthy self-interest.* Get out your sticky notes to make a reminder for your mirror or use a marker and ribbon for a bracelet and write this new mantra, *plug the energy drain*. This will remind you that you have a choice.

The people you stop enabling may make increased demands on you as you ply your new strong limit-setting, but they may actually evolve to a healthier place when you no longer accept their dependency on you

There Will Be Losses

As you go through the process of setting boundaries, you may want to look at the secondary gains you received from these nice but needy folks. Did they help you feel important with resources others could depend upon? Did you believe you needed to always give to people to be liked or loved? That was true for me. Growing up with a depressed, dependent mother, I was hugely attracted to needy friends and romantic partners I could help and coach, but the experience was tremendously frustrating. I learned that these immature, dependent people wanted to keep me as their strong caregiver and rarely used my support to grow up. To change these patterns it's necessary to reduce your offers of advice in a loving way and not routinely respond to needs and problems.

Don't Give Up Your Power

Sometimes you may be so skillful in reading a man's signals and decoding his subtle messages that you can become exactly what he wants in a woman. This type of sexual power can be very intoxicating for women, and many movies and television shows reflect these images. However, it's dangerous to use your highly evolved intuition this way since the façade will dissolve if the relationship continues. To support the growth of your authentic feminine nature tell yourself that there is no reason to pretend to be someone you aren't to get love and approval. When you are grounded in the truth of who and what you are, this way of getting attention will no longer be entertaining and may even feel distasteful.

Empathy Is Deep Listening

Now that you've detached from those uses of your sensitivity that exhaust you and drain your energy, I want to show you instead how to use your beautiful, deep, feeling nature as a gift to those you cherish and want to be close to. Compassion is frequently taken for empathy but it is somewhat different. Compassion is feeling *for* someone, having sympathy or understanding for their plight. Empathy is about feeling *with* someone—allowing yourself to get into their experience and sharing their suffering or excitement as if it was your own. It's about removing the barriers like criticism, judgment, righteousness, superiority, and other positions that separate you from your partner, that get in the way of this connecting. Empathy includes active listening, a communication tool for setting opinions and filters aside and understanding another's words and ideas, which was introduced in Chapter 7. It also includes mirroring, which is recognizing and validating another's feelings. Empathy is not always communicated with words. There is nonverbal empathy which is sometimes the best or only kind needed. Nonverbal empathy is a touch like a pat on the shoulder, a hand squeeze, a hug, or in some cases just being there, allowing your eyes to communicate that which might be impossible to say with words.

Empathy Can Be Learned

Active listening may be a term that is more familiar to you than empathy. It is routinely taught in most communication classes as well as business applications, parenting, and couples' workshops as a way to really listen and get what another is saying without judgments and filters. When practicing active listening, you basically set aside your own positions and feelings and listen intently to your partner. You take in and understand whatever he's conveying, wanting, and needing. The only responses you give are ones that confirm what you heard or sensed about their communication. It is not an exchange of ideas, nor a debate or negotiation and there is no need to agree or resolve a problem. Empathy can go further and, as you pick up in the tone or nonverbal cues—the underlying emotions and feelings that your partner is communicating—you may actually be able to identify with them and connect to a time when you felt this way. While everyone can learn active listening and it is appropriate for most settings, empathy presumes more intimacy, and is something that is reserved for people who matter to you. Empathy is often a spontaneous experience when you are attuned to someone and resonate emotionally with them.

Many people who have received empathetic listening in a therapy session realize that being heard this way is not something they have experienced often. It is how you give yourself to another, particularly someone you care about. When you are empathic with your partner, you set aside whatever you think or believe and use your own emotional center to resonate with what he is saying and feeling. It is ideal for both partners to communicate this way with each other, but you may still benefit even if it is not reciprocated.

Use Active Listening to Defuse an Argument

In most arguments two people are trying to be heard, understood, and validated, and no one may be listening. The argument continues with escalating furor, each partner holding the intention of winning, being right, and convincing the other person of his or her position. The argument usually ends without resolution and residual anger, resentment, and hurt feelings continue afterward. With active listening, where one partner is actually carefully listening and giving feedback that the information was received, there often can be closeness even if the conflict is not resolved.

Men usually have a much more difficult time with active listening and empathic communication than women. Either because of their nature or socialization, men usually need practice to suspend their own analytical, logical, and judgmental mind and be receptive to not just the words but the feelings and tone of what is being conveyed. Even though your man may not have any interest or ability to learn active listening and empathy, using it with him will still be useful.

 My guy seems not to have many feelings to empathize with. Could he be what I would call a "head person" and just have thoughts?—*Tricia*

DEAR TRICIA: Focus on his thoughts then, and it may trigger a hint of his deeply buried feelings. If you pay attention, sometimes you will see that a thought is actually a feeling in disguise.

Empathy May Not Be Reciprocated

Heather, forty-three, remembers her attempt to enlist Paul in couples' counseling with active listening communication as the objective. Heather thought that if she and Paul could actually hear what the other was saying, then their problems would be resolved. However, they found that they could follow instructions in the sessions, but in their own home environment this technique went out the window and they fell back into their customary shouting matches. When I suggested to Heather that she use active listening or even empathy when in a discussion with Paul, she objected the way you may object. "If he isn't able or willing to be that way with me, why should I be with him?"

I told Heather that Paul may never learn or use these tools, or he may eventually understand their value from his experience with her. However, Heather should practice them so she can understand Paul's position and begin to accept him and create closeness rather than conflict. I give that same advice to you: use active listening or empathy in your relationship as a way to create peace for yourself and harmony in your home. Its purpose is not to teach, coach, or change your partner.

Women usually report that, when the arguments cease and they can hear, take in, and validate their partner's response, one of two things happens. Your partner may be able to see the flaws in his own position as it is explored fully, or he may be softened by your interest and understanding of his position and become willing to compromise or give in. Oftentimes, when we are truly heard the fight goes out of us. However, avoid falling into the give-to-get school of relationships that we've previously discussed. You'll only feel resentful if you give to get and end up not getting. Not having expectations but giving because it benefits you as well as him is the right orientation for empathy.

Practice Empathy

Heather reported that it was easy for her to be empathic with Paul when there was no conflict. When he shared with her some concerns he was having with his grown son, or with work pressures, she could listen and support him, and suspend any need to advise, help, or fix the situation. This attention, without any agenda of her own, helped him open up to his feelings and he remarked afterward that he could share thoughts and emotions he didn't even know he had until he spoke aloud about them to her. However, when Paul was angry it was much more difficult for Heather to stay open and really listen to him.

Paul often criticized Heather's management of Ariel, her daughter from a previous marriage. When Heather defended her decisions or Ariel's behavior, it riled Paul even more and the couple ended up hurt, angry, and disconnected. Here's a transcript of the empathic roleplay Heather and I worked out in her session for her to use the next time one of the regular arguments with Paul surfaced.

PAUL (ME): I can't believe you're letting Ariel be on the phone all night when she got a D in math. What are you thinking? She's just twelve. She needs structure, and it's your job to provide it.

HEATHER: I hear you Paul. You're concerned I'm not providing enough structure for Ariel, that I'm letting her get away with being on the phone when she's got homework. Is that right?

PAUL (ME): Exactly. She's learning bad habits that are going to follow her. I don't know why you can't see it.

HEATHER: Ok, I'm getting it now. You want Ariel to develop better study habits. It's a worry for you.

PAUL (ME): Yes, aren't you worried when a seventh grader is on the verge of failing math?

HEATHER: You really care about her and want her to be successful. I appreciate that. I see that you're being supportive and caring. I understand now your feelings and I'm going to work on this.

After our roleplay, Heather expressed amazement. "This isn't how it would have gone before. I would have gotten defensive and rebutted what felt like an attack from Paul about my parenting, something I'm very sensitive about. My mom died when I was eight years old and I worry that I'm not the best mother. Now, I see how that defensive tact didn't allow Paul to fully express himself because I cut him off and shut him down. I really like what we did here. I'm going to try it."

Mirroring Is a Part of Empathy

Mirroring—which Heather used to recognize and validate Paul's feelings—is vitally important to children, but most of us didn't receive enough of it. Mirroring is that part of empathy where feelings are validated. It is reflecting back like a mirror the child's expression so that the child grasps for him or herself what he or she is feeling. It is how we learn to understand our own emotions and read the data that they give us. Men are apt to have their emotions blocked and as children they are routinely encouraged to deny or repress their feelings in the interest of masculinity. Instead of reflecting their disappointment or sadness with supportive statements like, *of course you're angry or upset to strike out, it's okay to cry or be mad,* or *I'll hug you if you like,* they are usually told in a gruff voice, *suck it up, blow it off, don't embarrass yourself, don't be a wuss.* Fortunately, this is beginning to change and enlightened parents and educators are recognizing that pushing emotions underground cuts the connection that people have with their intuition and inner selves, and eliminates a rich source of data. Stuffing emotions makes it hard to capture how you feel and reduces your ability to connect deeply with others.

Keep in mind that empathy includes both mirroring (recognizing and reflecting feelings), and active listening (setting your own filters and opinions aside so you can understand fully what someone is saying). It sometimes is possible to feel the emotions your partner may be expressing as well. Offering empathy can make up for what many people did not receive as children and offers a way for them to better understand themselves now.

How to Use Empathy

Empathy is not something you can always give. When your defensiveness and anger are triggered, it is wise to table the conversation until you can be undefended and present. Tell your partner: *I am finding it hard to take in what you are saying to me. I would like to have this conversation when I feel calm and receptive.* Then be clear about not going forward when you know the outcome will not be positive.

Complications arise when you are unable to stay in that place of openness and presence and practice methods other than empathy, active listening, or mirroring. The impetus to teach, coach, correct, or offer alternate or opposing viewpoints is not empathic. It is also not empathic to close down the discussion by labeling, judging, or offering solutions.

 My husband is angry a lot. When do I respond with empathy and when do I make a fast exit and wait for him to cool down?—*Dottie*

DEAR DOTTIE: Give up for a time if his anger is just dumping or a defense that you can't penetrate. You'll recognize stonewalling if he is not responsive to anything you say. Later when he's calm you could ask if he wants to talk about it.

Clients often ask me how to handle an exchange when they don't agree, when what their man is saying is totally unacceptable to them. In that case, it's best to wait until another time to express your feelings and needs about the problem. For now, perhaps you can say with honesty that you can understand his position, feelings, and where he is coming from.

Empathy Can Benefit Both of You

Men, on the whole, have been socialized to appear tough or to deny their emotions. In our culture, anger is a socially acceptable emotion for a man to show and using anger or a bullying tactic is often how men get their way—especially with women. Men, programmed as they are to be competitive, will often muster a counterattack to what they perceive to be a challenge. But, by practicing empathy, you may discover that most men have other feelings that are not close to the surface or readily available that may come out if they feel safe to reveal them.

At her last visit with me, Heather reported that she could sometimes handle a conflict with Paul by staying open and empathic. She noticed that when she *got* Paul and realized his positive intentions even though his voice was rough and attacking at first, she did feel more understanding and experienced an open heart for him; she took a loving feeling away from their exchange. Heather realized, as you may also come to understand, that she could strongly connect and truly join with Paul by totally getting him, appreciating his struggle, and understanding that his childhood wounding may still be manifesting in the present. Ideally, this would work both ways, but even if you are the giver and your man is not able to reciprocate, the fact the he allows you to connect to him in this way can make the experience in some sense complete for you.

Lead by Example

You may be saying, *Hey wait a minute—when do I get to say my piece, give my side, and get my position validated?* Well, that may

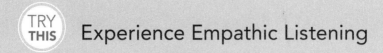

Experience Empathic Listening

1 Identify some issues in your relationship and find a time to experiment with listening. It may at first be just a one-sentence response that demonstrates active listening or empathy.

2 What surprises or discoveries did you make about your man as a result of using active listening or empathy?

3 How have you been able to defuse conflict by taking an empathic approach?

happen, but then again it may not. If you want to talk about something with your partner, it's a good idea is to identify a time to discuss it rather than blindside him with it. There may be a better outcome if you say, for example, *after dinner tonight I want to talk to you about something, is that a good time for you?* Then, when you start the conversation, describe what you want from him. *I want to tell you how I feel about this matter and it's important that you just listen to me.* If he starts to interject or begins to argue, say something like, *I know you don't agree or see things the same way, but for now could you just understand where I am coming from? Could you tell me back what I said so I know you are really getting my side to this?*

This may or may not work. If he is unwilling or unable to listen to your viewpoint, you could give him an empathic response like, *are you telling me that you don't want to know what I think and feel, that it's not important to you to understand my position? That's what I'm getting from you. Is that true?*

Consider YOUR Mindset As a woman, particularly if you grew up in a dysfunctional household, you may be too sensitive and use up a lot of your emotional energy with people who exhaust you and return little in the way of real nurturing. It may be necessary to begin setting limits and boundaries and reducing some of these energy drains so that you'll have the ability to connect empathically with the people who matter most. Empathy takes you a step beyond active listening where you not only get the ideas and content being communicated but join with the emotions as well. Mirroring, which can be a part of empathy, is important for children but can also be a useful tool for recognizing and validating your partner's feelings. While your man may not be able to reciprocate in kind, practicing empathy with him may help you understand him better, defuse conflict, and increase closeness. There is also the possibility that he may be able to follow your lead.

Share YOUR Views *Discuss this chapter in your book club or women's circle, or with friends:*

1 Have you had formal instruction in active listening through a business, parenting, or relationship class? Was it easy to implement and practice on your own? What skills do you continue to use?

2 Have you noticed that your sensitivity makes you too aware of other people's needs and feeling? Do you feel guilty if you don't respond to them?

3 How do you feel about "leading by example" when using empathy? Do you think it would be helpful or do you have some resistance to trying it?

PART THREE

THE CONTENTED MINDSET

Your relationship can't be your "everything," and you need to learn about yourself and take some risks to expand your life in the direction of your dreams. Being aware of the present and learning to awaken your senses to your immediate, sometimes wonderful, sometimes stressful life, will help you resist the make-believe world of the past or future. A good supply of energy is necessary to feel good and accomplish all that is important in your life and relationship and learning to manage it well is essential. Developing your own inner resources and ability to soothe and support yourself will make you ultimately more autonomous and empowered. Throughout this section, you'll find many examples to convince you that you can make the changes and achieve the same results as the people profiled. Looking at the elements you and your partner bring to your relationship and choosing among the many options will expand your vision and help you realize that there is more than one way to fit together.

CHAPTER 10

ONE SIZE FITS NO ONE

There are as many different kinds of relationships as there are people who form them. Allowing yourself to consider all the ways that people come together and support and nurture each other will expand your vision of your relationship and make it possible for you to see the options in your own partnership. Your idea of a good relationship may have come from growing up with parents who related to each other affectionately and respectfully, but it may also have come from not seeing a healthy relationship modeled. If this is the case, you may idealize something that is not attainable or is just one version of many possibilities. Everyone continually grows and changes and a good relationship needs to be a fluid and flexible container—shaped and honed by the experiences the couple have shared together and the way they have evolved. A codependent relationship forms when one or both partners have needs and expectations of the relationship and attempt to create a partnership that thwarts this lively growth, fearful that change may bring about something they won't like. A relationship must be approached as an adventure like traveling in a foreign country where new things requiring innovative solutions are presented at every turn.

There are certain givens in a partnership that may not be negotiable so there may be things to work with that are not ideal and require sacrifice and compromise. Each couple has the responsibility to find their own pattern of togetherness, one that suits them, and not compare themselves to what others have created or to a fantasy. Successful couples allow each other a generous amount of room and support each other's dreams regardless of the effect on their own needs and interests.

Create a Relationship Container

Imagine that you're in a relationship design center with an almost unlimited array of choices and patterns—just like the endless samples of paint, fabric, flooring, and decorating elements available for your home. You're here because you want to create a real place for your relationship to live, an arrangement that satisfies your most important needs and desires. In this setting you have the ability and the tools to determine what style of relationship will fit you and your man and to create a relationship container that uniquely meets your needs. The requirements of even a generation ago are gone. You no longer have to contort yourself within the simplistic model of a single lifetime relationship; you don't have to marry the boy next door, buy a house in the same small town, raise three children, cook chuck roast every Sunday, get matching rocking chairs, and end up with a joint headstone in the local cemetery.

The only problem is that you don't get to decide everything. The limits you have to work within are created by who you each are and the constant kaleidoscope of changing values, unfolding lives, and shifting needs and ideas. As you know, there will always be change, and problems and conflicts will arise when you try to keep things constant. There will always be open-ended explorations, negotiations, and decisions as you journey through life with your partner and work with the creative elements and events that present themselves. Nothing will ever be static.

 My live-in boyfriend and I have a little girl together and parent his son by his ex-wife on weekends. How do I respond to my family who is pressuring us to marry? —*Ashley*

DEAR ASHLEY: Are you sure it isn't you wanting marriage and using your family to pressure him? In either case, leave your family out of it and express directly to him what you want.

Avoid Codependence

Your primary relationship will evolve over time as you allow and encourage both yourself and your partner to fully become who you are, and to grow in the ways that are most important. Codependence—where two people attempt to control each other and function as one dysfunctional unit—inhibits this growth. In this type of a relationship, there is the erroneous belief that one's happiness and success as a couple is dependent on how the other partner feels and behaves. There is also usually a high degree of conflict because there are constant demands to conform to the expectations of the other. To stay together, change is thwarted and both partners may feel stifled. The relationship can become lifeless and monotonous with the only excitement generated by the strife of attacks and counterattacks and possibly breaking up and making up.

In a typical codependent relationship, the woman will do most of the conforming and will submerge her feelings and needs in deference to her man. Abandonment issues may be at the core when someone makes this choice, and the resulting feelings of

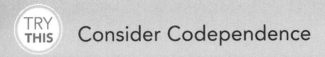

Consider Codependence

1 Identify ways that you want your man to change. What behaviors do you complain or nag him about?

2 Ask yourself if you're moving your relationship in the direction of codependence. Are you coaching your partner to become what you want him to be, causing him to submerge his authentic self?

3 How might you be resisting your own growth and making your partner's needs more important?

4 Do you have feelings of anger or resentment that you're not expressing, that come out as depression, because you are giving up yourself to please your partner?

anger and resentment may simmer under the surface or manifest instead as chronic depression. This was the case with Norma, thirty-five, and her live-in boyfriend, Jack. Norma's parents divorced when she was eleven and her father rarely saw her. She remembered his long-distance phone calls, the occasional gift of clothing that didn't fit, and the awkward visits. Her mother had a series of boyfriends, married and divorced another husband, and never had time for Norma. Now Norma, having felt abandoned by both parents, is hyper-vigilant about Jack, constantly monitoring his actions and behaviors, testing his love to see if he will choose to be with her over other options, watching his every move suspiciously. She believes that she must become what Jack wants to strengthen the relationship and, in her efforts to please him, she is often seeking his feedback and advice about every-day things like how to style her hair, what to cook for dinner, and even how to deal with clients at her job. Because she is so sensitive to Jack's reactions, he is becoming cautious about what he says to keep from upsetting her. Most of their conflicts stem from him not responding the way she wants, or being indifferent to her needs of him. When Norma first came to see me she was troubled by mood swings, but mostly depression, as she imagined Jack was not as caring as she wanted. This is a codependent rela-tionship in the making.

Earmarks of a Healthy Relationship

In a healthy relationship there is encouragement and freedom that allows each person to evolve naturally, even if it does not always meet the needs of the other partners. Since each person is an individual and brings his or her complete personality to the union, there will be situations where one or the other is uncom-fortable or disturbed by the change. As was previously discussed, difficulties will frequently stimulate character development and may create a higher degree of interest in the relationship. How-ever, there is also the risk that your partner will be unable to rise to the challenge and will threaten to leave. You may know of someone who has experienced this type of emotional blackmail where a controlling, fragile, or self-serving partner will attempt to extort their mate under the threat of leaving without regard to the other's needs and feelings. This presents a thorny dilemma that doesn't have an easy solution.

Relationships where the partners give each other a generous amount of room will be livelier with more excitement. Partners may find each other difficult, but also more enjoyable and interesting. When one partner grows there can be a resulting growth, perhaps of a different kind, in the other partner. At the basis of this kind of partnership is a profound respect for who each other is, needs to be, and dreams of becoming. You want no less for your partner than what you want for yourself—the opportunity and support to live life to the fullest, to respond to the challenge of your life's purpose and your most cherished dreams, and to rise to whatever it is you're called to do. This is the basis for true love and the opposite of what fragile codependents desire: *I want you to be what I need so I don't have to feel bad, or only change in ways that make life good for me.*

Norma resisted my suggestion that Jack may not be the problem, that she could make some changes in herself and then consider whether there was something that needed to be fixed in the relationship. She had an idea of how a good relationship should be, not based on any direct experience, but as a reaction to what she was exposed to as a child. Norma wanted to become the opposite of her mother to make sure this relationship with Jack lasts. For starters, I asked Norma to consider that maybe she had some of the same character traits she saw in her mother.

"It can't be," She said. "My mother was totally self-absorbed, always interested in how she looked, focused on whatever guy she was dating at the time, and I felt like a third wheel. I'm nothing like her!"

I reassured Norma that I was not blaming her or her mother, but was trying to understand what she took away from her formative years, what she saw in the way her mother related to men. After awhile she began to recognize that like herself, her mother was chronically unhappy and depressed. There was a lot of conflict and arguing between her mother and her boyfriends and second husband. Norma realized that her mother had high control needs and wanted things her way. Norma recalled, "In many ways she was a *queen* and had impossible expectations." In further

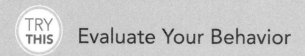

TRY THIS   Evaluate Your Behavior

1   Do you have expectations about your partner or the relationship that are unrealistic or that are difficult for him to meet?

2   Can you see how making changes for yourself can change your relationship even if your partner does not change?

3   Are there ways that you are keeping yourself stuck to please your partner or to make your relationship work that are not in your best interest?

discussions Norma saw that her mother's inability to sustain a relationship may have been because she needed too much from men; she made them the reason for her happiness or her disappointment. We talked about how Norma might need too much attention from Jack, that she is trying too hard to make sure they stay together. Like her mother, she may be too focused on getting Jack to be what she needs and not allowing him to have his own reactions. She described it this way: *I'm realizing that being glued together won't work in the long term. I was trying to keep Jack and me glued together. There has to be space for each of us to be ourselves.*

Healthy Partnerships Can Come in Different Forms

When strong, equal, evolved partners come together they create a lifestyle and a relationship that may not be like those of anyone else they know. This way of living requires the attitude that the partners do not need to contort themselves to fit into a certain pattern. In my practice I have seen every kind of relationship, but the ones that have survived and grown in connection and respect have had the willingness to look beyond the commonplace and create what worked for them.

One couple I worked with had teenage children when they married and moved their families together, but soon realized that a blended family was too conflicted and difficult for them to manage. Despite the confusion and consternation of families and friends, they decided to live separately with their children and do things together on the weeks when their ex-spouses had child duty with the long-range plan to have one home again when the children were emancipated. Another client's husband was offered a relocation package when his job ended, but she could not consider moving away when their young disabled daughter had finally gotten established with the necessary services. Now he commutes on weekends until something can be worked out. Maybe you know someone who must spend several weeks out of the month caring for an elderly relative, requiring her spouse to be a bachelor during those times. In an economic downturn, two sisters and their husbands decided to buy a large house together and pool their resources when neither couple had the capability on their own to do it and now are working out how to live together amicably. Another couple decided to take in two roommates when financial reverses made it impossible to keep their house otherwise.

Even within the seemingly traditional partnership there are numerous variations. Clients of mine have volunteered abroad, taken a month-long workshop, completed a degree program in a distant location, or lived with extended family members. In a healthy union the relationship container is resilient and strong enough to allow for unique variations.

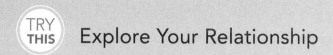

Explore Your Relationship

1. What desire do you have that is frustrated by your belief that your partner wouldn't like or approve of it?

2. What fears would you have if you allowed your partner freedom to pursue his dreams?

3. How is your partnership unique? How is it different from the norm that you formerly believed?

Negotiate Your Relationship

Even within a relationship, what people want and how they negotiate their needs is important. Conflict arises when one partner wants or expects something that the other partner is unable or unwilling to give. Sex is a good example since in many relationships the frequency of intimacy does not match the desire of one of the partners. The type and variation of sexual behaviors may also be at odds. Often issues like sex are not a problem of communication as some women may think. They erroneously believe that if their partners truly understood their needs, the problem would be resolved. Instead, the problem is that both partners do not have identical needs and interests and it requires a high degree of acceptance and understanding to solve the problem, rather than anger, verbal attacks, and threats.

There is no guarantee in a relationship that all of your needs and desires will be fulfilled. It is immature to believe that your partner is responsible for satisfying your desires. Couple's counseling may help to address ways of becoming more compatible, but you need to realize that an impasse may exist and acceptance may be the only resolution.

Accommodate Differences

Differences in a relationship can present thorny dilemmas and difficult times where negotiation and adjustment are required. It is rare—and undesirable—to find partners who are always confluent and in agreement. Differences offer more growth possibilities and the process of working them out can actually increase a couple's respect and love for each other. You may know people who have met many hardships, or dealt with tragedies and loss, and came through it with a stronger bond. It helps to see a balance between what you must relinquish and what you are getting in return. Sometimes that isn't clear at first and it may take some time and patience until new patterns form and problems dissipate. Being open and expressing your feelings honestly without blame or anger is the best way to put things on the table and begin generating options.

 My ex had an affair and now I'm very suspicious of my fiancé cheating on me. Is it ok that I spy on his cell phone and e-mail and always have to know everything he does?—*Dana*

DEAR DANA: You think these tactics will help you, but they will eventually create more distrust. You may need a therapist to help you work through the anxiety that has you both in a stranglehold.

You may feel a range of emotions including disappointment, sadness, or grief when it becomes clear that your mate is unable to supply you with all you want in the relationship. This was the situation with Betsy when Kyle did not share her devotion to a nonprofit organization where she was the board president. Since they were a childless professional couple, he could accept weekdays where she was mostly unavailable if on the weekends she would make time for them to do things together. They agreed to plan their own eating schedules during the week when Betsy was busy with her charity and Kyle was less so, and then on weekends arrange meals that they both enjoyed. Kyle began working out and getting fit which Betsy found attractive but she also felt threatened that he might get attention from sexy young women. Despite her busy schedule she found herself more interested in sex with him now on the weekends. Eventually Kyle was able to support her fundraisers and social events and together they discovered more passion and closeness even with the time apart.

It was different with Marilyn and Jerry. When they first met, Marilyn was attracted to Jerry's sexual appetite. He had been in a sexless marriage before his divorce, and initially he couldn't get enough of Marilyn. She reported beautiful weekends in Monterey and Napa at little inns and boutique hotels where they had impossibly romantic times. He would order dual massages and flowers and champagne for their room and they were both surprised and grateful that they could have such wonderful sex in their fifties.

All that changed when Jerry was diagnosed with diabetes and high blood pressure and experienced his first bouts of sexual dysfunction. He had difficulty talking about it with Marilyn and was reluctant to seek a medical consultation, but when he did the outcome was disappointing. Apparently he was not a good candidate for the newer drugs for this problem and the physical methods for sustaining an erection were uncomfortable for him to use. Despite Marilyn's reassurance and encouragement, at age fifty-seven Jerry decided that sex for him was a thing of the past. Because he was so conditioned to associate touching and affection with sex, those behaviors also became infrequent, and when

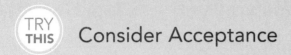

1   What is an element of your relationship that has created
    conflict but is difficult or impossible to resolve?

2   What are you being asked to accept? How might you adapt
    to something different?

3   How might you grow by learning to live with a variation?
    What are your feelings about this?

Marilyn initiated cuddling and closeness, he complained she was pressuring him for sex. Reluctantly, Marilyn accepted that sex was over as they once knew it, but gradually introduced Jerry to her vibrator and enlisted his help in giving her an orgasm, a reasonable substitute, but the best part was the cuddling and affection that now came back into their new style of lovemaking.

Explore Styles of Relating

There are many different ways that people engage with each other based on their personalities, life conditioning, and their ideas about relationships. There is the distinct probability that the partners in any relationship will have different preferences that will require negotiating. My reason for describing these three broad styles is to stimulate your thinking so that you and your partner can fill in the details and find a way to relate that is just right for you. Without comparing yourself to an ideal or to what others may have, you can be content in the knowledge that what you have designed is uniquely yours—but remember that as your needs change so may your relationship style.

If there's a disconnect and you recognize it as occurring due to dissimilar preferences, acceptance is the best way of resolving it. Since you have many ways of meeting your needs, you won't look to your significant other as the only choice.

Face-to-Face Style

This style is called face-to-face, not because of the way the partners are positioned as they relate, but as a metaphor which illustrates a direct open way of communicating. It assumes that both people are willing to share deeply of themselves. A lot of women prefer a face-to-face style of relating, which is one of profound intimacy and interpersonal risk-taking. The real intimacy occurs in the realm of communication where the partners can create the safety necessary to honestly reveal their deep feelings and experiences. There can also be sexual intimacy with a high degree of trust and desires can be discussed and explored in a climate of acceptance.

Some women believe that this is the only way a couple can relate, that this is the norm. You may have grown up seeing your parents with a close and communicative connection, but you may also have grown up in a dysfunctional family and idealized that the honest open expression of feelings and needs is what good relationships are about. It can be a beautiful experience and create an amazing bond when a woman finds a man willing and available for this kind of relating, but it can be a source of conflict when a woman struggles to form a face-to-face connection with a man who is not able to be this open. In cases where a woman desires this type of verbal intimacy and is with a man who is uncomfortable with it, it would be important for her to develop friendships where sharing in this dimension is possible. There are also growth groups of various kinds that create a safe space for people to share intimately with each other. To expect this in our primary relationship is to court unnecessary conflict and disappointment.

Side-by-Side Style

Couples who prefer a side-by-side style of relating to one another see doing things together as the basis for a good relationship. They like the camaraderie and companionship of their partner—who they think of as a buddy—during outdoor activities, spectator sports, shared hobbies, or even while doing things as simple as watching TV, or playing video or card games. All relationships may include companionship in some form but there are those relationships that have this element at the core. These kinds of relationships rarely touch on the deeper aspects of feelings or ideas and focus instead on the practical concrete aspects of life together like grocery shopping or cooking together. Side-by-side couples may not desire as much intimacy and often have fun visiting or traveling with other couples and spending time hanging out with friends. For example, many parents find that their children's friends offer them activities with other families when their opportunities for time alone together is reduced.

 Ask Sally My husband complains that I won't try new things that he wants to do like snowboarding or biking. I don't like being cold, wet, or uncomfortable. What do I do?—*Kelly*

DEAR KELLY: You have three choices here—you can be okay with him finding a buddy to play with, or you can put up with the discomfort. The third choice—sulking, pouting, and complaining to keep him home—is a no-no.

Back-to-Back Style

Those with a back-to-back style of relating may end up in a union where each partner is very independent and functions semi-autonomously. The image is of both partners supporting each other while looking out in opposite directions. Despite the fact that these partners may spend less time together than other couples, their interest, excitement, and love for each may be even more intense because of the richness they each bring to their union. Frequently, partners with this style of relating will tell me that they know that their partner is there for them when they need it, and that although they are afforded a lot of autonomy, they have great trust for each other as well. Their commitment to each other may be high despite perhaps living apart or having other compelling interests.

Marilyn had problems with Jerry's need for her to do things together—camping in his motor home, endless rounds of golf, and just sitting together holding hands at night on the couch watching rented movies. She saw him as needy and clingy and dependent on her but actually this was just a style of relating he had had in his previous relationship and preferred. Marilyn was independent and did not desire as much closeness. She was geared for the back-to-back style of relating, which has each partner facing out in their own different worlds and sharing only a little at the edges. They each may have demanding big jobs, be engrossed in getting an education, have interests that require a lot of time and attention, or just be of an introverted personality type that requires less interaction. Of course these are just broad examples and within these categories are unlimited variations and possibilities. Like Marilyn and Jerry, you may find that your relationship requires some flexibility and negotiating.

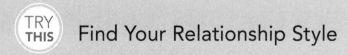

Find Your Relationship Style

1 How are you and your partner the same or different in your relationship preferences?

2 What changes could you make in your beliefs that would allow your relationship to be fine the way it is? What style works for the two of you?

3 In what ways might your relationship need breathing room, more space?

4 Is there social pressure and disapproval from others that keep you from exploring relationship options that would be a better fit for you?

Consider YOUR Mindset Now that you are realizing all the possibilities and limitations in your relationship design center, it is incumbent on you to see whether the changes need to be made only in your own head or whether there are actual changes you can make that would create an allowing space for you and your man to best express yourselves and your love. Some changes can be shifts in the way you view yourself, your partner, and your relationship. Other changes will take some negotiating, or a different way of being. The overarching intent of these practices is to reduce the conflict and increase the connection between you and your partner. It is useful to see that every relationship needs a container, a metaphorical place that is constructed by your beliefs, feelings, and values. By becoming honest, facing your fears, and opening to change you have the ability to create such a place that will uniquely fit your current needs and evolve as you and your partner grow.

Share YOUR Views *Discuss this chapter in your book club or women's circle, or with friends:*

1 Does it seem to you that younger women are seeing more options for themselves and can restyle their relationships and life choices to be a better fit for them than generations past? How is that true or not true for you?

2 What have you had to adjust to in your relationship that has been difficult or demanding? What bumps in the road have required some negotiating and acceptance for you?

3 Do you believe codependent relationships are confining and conflicted or do you think that it's necessary for partners to shape themselves and their aspirations to be in sync with each other?

CHAPTER 11

YOUR LIFE—REV IT UP!

Women's dreams and goals for their lives are often not well supported by partners and sometimes not even by themselves. While women are now holding down successful careers and maintaining friendships and hobbies, there are many who still see their primary role as nurturing others. If you're a baby boomer, you may have been conditioned to build a life around what was possible after the family had been looked after, so re-envisioning your goals may be even more challenging. While men were supported in education and careers, it was assumed that, for a woman, these would be of a lower priority than family needs. Fortunately, today's women are demonstrating the courage necessary to break out of this model and are verbalizing greater aspirations than being loved by a good man. Unfortunately, many women of every age still find it difficult to identify what they want for themselves, and don't know what to do with the energy that becomes available when the focus is no longer on the problems in the relationship. If this is the case with you, it may be necessary to work through your fears and anxieties that can sabotage taking even an initial step. To discover what ignites your passion and is ultimately fulfilling may require that you pay attention to faint stirrings, and begin trial and error explorations to find it.

You benefit when you risk expanding your vision for yourself, and your man may be positively affected as well. The energy in the relationship will be renewed and refreshed when you allow outside activities to nurture and enhance your good feelings about yourself. Also, the pressure on your man to be your "everything" may be reduced and may lighten up your experience together. He may even be challenged to grow himself and further enliven the relationship. There are risks, however, for a woman whose man is unable to embrace this infusion of new energy but even that sad realization will serve to inform her choices.

Explore the Possibilities

Imagine you are in a movie theater and the music and action are beginning. The camera is zooming in on your house and soon you realize that this is a story about you. Let's hope you don't find yourself complaining about how your man displeases you and everything you've tried to do to reform him. You don't want to see your day filled with the tedium of endless phone conversations, net surfing, mall excursions, and television. Instead, you want to be glued to your seat, cheering and celebrating this amazing and beautiful being who is inventing and reinventing herself before your eyes—a grounded, life-affirming feminine presence who speaks her truth and asks for what she wants. Because love is abundantly available to you, you don't need to contort and deny yourself to achieve it. Instead, you'll be leading your man, kids, friends—and even the world—by example. Feeling confident and good about yourself, you'll never have to manipulate others or misuse your sexual power. The woman you see on the screen is the woman who, in your heart, you know is you and the life unfolding in front of your eyes is the one you were born to live. I hope you are inspired and challenged and recognize that you are this potent.

Take Steps to More Passion

The movie was fun, but becoming that woman on the screen will have to start with some baby steps. Now that you've been experiencing increased energy and time as a result of not focusing on problems and having fewer arguments, you will want to create something wonderful for yourself out of that power. The positive attitude that comes from focusing on goals and dreams instead of problems will become a real source of energy. Getting on with your own life—whether your partner changes or not—will empower you to think outside the relationship.

You will discover the motivation and drive to take risks, try new activities, and uncover the latent dreams that were put on the back burner. Some may be merely fun, like getting a new hair color or updating your wardrobe. Others might be social like joining a book club. Important ones like going back to school, applying for a new job, or making a commitment to get in shape may also surface.

 Ask Sally I only ever wanted to be a wife and mom. Now I'm realizing that it burdens my husband and kids to need them to be my whole life. Where do I start?—*Meghan*

DEAR MEGHAN: Obviously you've already started with this new idea. It's not easy and may take some time to break out, but experiment with a class, group, or part-time job.

When you accept the challenge to be yourself, you recognize that your relationship—even if it's a great one—cannot be all that you want and need. Experts estimate that only about 25 percent of your fulfillment should come from a relationship. A full life includes many aspects—a wide range of nurturing activities, people, events, new skills and abilities—as you explore what pleasures and satisfies you.

Fan the Sparks of Interest

Kendra brought the results of this exercise into a session with me. She had identified several significant events in her life but we'll just discuss two of them here. When Kendra was nine, she took gymnastic classes from a young male teacher who she loved and wanted to please. The words that were generated from this experience included: confident, coordinated, belonging, proud, accomplished, successful, and special. Her sentences were: *I liked the feeling of belonging to a group and being successful. It made me confident when I accomplished hard tasks. I am coordinated and am proud of my athletic ability.*

Another event that stood out for her was working on the high school newspaper and getting an award for an essay. She was called up on stage at an assembly where she was given a certificate and a cash prize by the local newspaper who published her piece. The words that flowed from this memory were excited, recognized, achievement, expressive, known, smart, capable, and creative. The sentences she formed using these words were: *I like having my achievements recognized. I want to be known as smart and capable. It's exciting to be recognized for being expressive and creative.*

To help Kendra work with these ideas, I asked her to sit with the energy that was stimulated by this exercise and see what came up for her. She said, "Belonging is big for me. I think I am beginning to realize that being a part of something outside my family gave me a lot of good feelings about myself and I don't have that now. Being in a structured program challenged me too and pushed me to do hard things which make me confident."

Find Sparks of Interest

This exercise may take time and you might want to do it over several days. It can yield some surprising and interesting ideas about your dreams and needs. It is based on events and experiences that you found satisfying and rewarding in your past. Dig around in those memories and mine the nuggets of truth that will point you to something new that will be similarly satisfying.

1 Beginning with birth, divide your life into five-year increments until you reach your present age. For each time period, identify one or two experiences that made you feel wonderful, excited, fulfilled, aglow, or successful. It's fine if some periods have several of these experiences and others none. Take your time and allow yourself to fully experience each phase in your life—the places where you lived, the houses you lived in, the people who were part of your life, the accomplishments that made you proud, and so on.

2 Go back to each of these fulfilling and satisfying experiences and relive them as vividly as you can, soaking up the sights, smells, feelings, and action. Quickly write down as many words as you can think of for each scene, for example: needed, valued, special, smart, and so forth.

3 Take the words you have generated and make new sentences about what you know or have learned about yourself and what may be important for you.

4 What new things do you want in your life that reflect the values that you've uncovered?

When I saw Kendra again, she had thought a lot about this exercise. She told me about her job that she didn't find particularly rewarding, but worked because the hours fit her family's schedule. Being obsessive about keeping up the house, making healthy meals, and getting the kids to their activities consumed her time and energy and she felt too tired for much else. Does this sound familiar? A lot of women tell me something similar. I asked Kendra what I am asking you: What would you want to try if you had the time and energy? What dreams do you have?

Kendra decided that she would love to be on a sports team—ladies' volleyball, basketball, or softball—like she had been earlier in her life. She was also considering taking a class in journalism or theater arts at the junior college just for fun. I encouraged Kendra to test out these ideas and to scale back her household duties to make the time. While her husband was willing to help she frequently rejected his offers because his way of helping didn't meet her standards but now she was considering how he could help her find some time to pursue one or both of these ideas. Kendra sent me an e-mail several months later and said that she was enjoying her basketball team and that her husband and the girls supported her games and were very proud of the points she scored. She said she couldn't possibly have predicted how much fun it could be or how basketball satisfied a need she hadn't even recognized before.

Women Can Recapture Dreams

Women often let life happen to them, and when caring for others fills up their time, they don't often step back to see how they can create the space and energy they need to take care of themselves. However, when you focus on your own needs and desires—those individual pursuits that draw you and spark your interest—you tell the truth about who you are in the deepest part of your being and what you need to bring that self fully into realization. You decide to matter to yourself even if there is no one to support you in these subtle desires that manifest in your consciousness. What initially was a fleeting thought can gain momentum and can begin to bloom into something necessary and important to your life.

This was how it was for Brie when she refocused her thoughts on her own life and what she always wanted instead of finding fault with her boyfriend. She described how she rescued dogs since she was a teen and volunteered with the SPCA. She felt the most abandoned and rejected by her dad when he moved away and started a new family, and she could identify with those scared dogs.

I probed Brie about where she was going with this, what she was beginning to understand about her needs now. "Well, this is an idea that's been hatching in my mind for awhile now. I want to be involved with children. It's not that Michael and I can't have kids of our own. We haven't tried yet. I want to help a child. I'm a third grade teacher; I love kids. I think I could offer something special to a child. I'm not sure what that would look like exactly—maybe volunteering in a program somewhere." Brie decided to fully explore that idea before broaching it with Michael. She checked out the kinds of kids and the processes involved and identified specifically where her heart wanted to take her.

Desires Need Encouragement to Bloom

Not everyone will have a fully formed desire. Most women need to sit with ideas and try things out to decide what activities will nurture them. It's usually best to begin with small projects or little goals. One of my clients decided to take a class in conversational Spanish to use on their frequent trips to Mexico and to volunteer at a clinic where Spanish-speaking women received family planning help. Another made a commitment to herself to finally get in shape whatever that would take. I've had others who renewed their participation in sports like tennis or volleyball that they had enjoyed in the past.

When you focus your attention on your own becoming, the direct route is often the best or only way to make something happen. When what you're reaching for is important to you— something that you dream of being, knowing, learning, or con- tributing—it's *your* responsibility to get these things for yourself. In most areas of your life, you may be the support person cham- pioning the goals and dreams of others, encouraging them to accomplish the things that are important to them. But when you say: *I want to go back to school, I want to play the saxophone again and join a community band, it's time I tried out for the little theater,* or *I'm starting a new business,* I hope you get the same level of enthusiasm and help that you have provided to them over the years—but don't depend on their approval and interest. You may have to find a way to take the beginning steps necessary to start the process without having your loved ones or even your partner onboard at first.

Don't Sabotage Yourself

Your own fear and anxiety may work to hold you back. It is possible to kill your own desire or dream without any feedback from others simply by telling yourself all the reasons why it's impractical, silly, or not workable. You may be overwhelming yourself with the size of your dream and not realize that even a large goal can have a first courageous—but oftentimes tiny—step that will test out your vision to see if it's truly what you want. A small new activity may create the positive energy to try some-

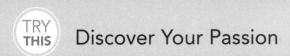

TRY THIS   Discover Your Passion

1   What do you want to be remembered for after you
    are gone?

2   What are those things that you have in the present that give
    your life meaning?

3   What do you envy about other women, what they are doing
    or becoming?

4   What stories do you read or hear about that most impress
    or inspire you?

5   What values are you living now or would like to live
    more fully?

thing more. It might just be tap dancing this year, but the energy
from doing something satisfying and enjoyable that's just for you
may prod you to tackle the bigger dream of going back to school
or signing up for a triathlon.

Self-Interest Is Healthy

You may believe that spending time, energy, and money on
things that are for your own satisfaction or pleasure is selfish.
Giving to others is so embedded in the female psyche that bad
feelings in the form of guilt and discomfort may arise when you

think of your own needs. Like some of my clients, you may have difficulty separating healthy self-interest from selfishness. The reason for this is that you got a lot of support and praise growing up when you put others' needs first. Practicing this pattern made you acutely aware of others' feelings and problems and as your energy was automatically drawn there it was harder for you to know what you wanted for yourself. Now, it is necessary for you to work through the neurotic guilt and support yourself as you grow in these new directions and attempt these risks. It calls on your inward strength to overcome the negativity of family members or even partners and push on to do what you believe is necessary for your spirit.

 My mother drummed it into me that, like her, I should be a self-sacrificing mom. How do I respond when she rolls her eyes, falls silent, or changes the subject if I talk about my needs?—*Tara*

DEAR TARA: Don't talk to her about your needs when all you get is disapproval. There are many ways to "leave home" and this is one. Love her but not her advice.

Get a Life

A healthy, mature adult sees getting a life as a wide array of choices with a primary relationship as a central focus but not the only focus. A satisfying existence includes friends who each add something, children and relatives who have a role to play, some kind of work that contributes to your sense of self, recreation, sports, fitness activities, clubs, groups, volunteer positions, or perhaps a religion or spiritual commitment. If you are reluctant to pursue some of these options and depend primarily on a relationship for many of your needs, then you may have some

Round Out Your Circle of People

1. Make a large circle on a full sheet of paper, put yourself as a dot in the middle, and then list the people in your life in relation to how close you are to them. Close to the center, name those with whom you are most intimate. At the outer edges, list the ones you are only acquainted with. In between put those in whom you have a moderate interest.

2. Decide if your people profile is adequate. Do you need more or fewer people in your life?

3. Would you like to increase your intimate circle or move some of those people to distant positions?

4. Are you too busy with people who don't provide any real nourishment?

5. Can you take more risks by increasing contact or reaching out to people you want to see more often?

issues leftover from childhood and be seeking a substitute parent. Individual counseling can be hugely beneficial if this is the case. Research consistently demonstrates that being socially connected to others contributes to both physical and mental health, and that you need relationships and people in your life for good self-esteem and to be able to deal with the normal stresses you will invariably encounter. While many women are extroverted, find it easy to relate to girlfriends, and are comfortable in many social situations, they may be expending too much energy with people who are not truly nurturing and may want to rethink their friendships. Introverted women who are more comfortable in small groups or one-on-one situations may need to coax themselves to reach out to others and accept more of the social possibilities that are being offered them.

Re-Energizing Yourself Benefits Both of You

Even if your relationship is great, it will benefit from time spent apart from your partner. Haven't you noticed that when you're apart for a few days, the spice is back when you are together again, that the time apart clears the staleness and sameness out of your relationship and freshens it again? When people are constantly together, their individual energies merge, and they often don't experience the same excitement or interest in each other that they feel after being apart. Taking time away from your partner renews your individual sexual energy and your physical connection becomes re-electrified, especially if the time apart is spent pursuing pleasurable activities.

Jane was totally exasperated with her alcoholic husband and was planning to leave him despite the upheaval it would cause herself and their college-aged sons. She was a computer programmer for the state but one of her dreams was to take a class in fiction writing and write a novel. I encouraged her to do this even though her focus each night was totally absorbed in whether her husband was drunk or sober.

To begin the process of moving on with her own separate life, she detached her energy from his addiction and concentrated on herself. She converted the guest room into an office and made it beautiful and pleasing for her emerging hobby. Every night, when her husband started drinking, she went there and worked on her online class in fiction writing. She became totally engrossed in the writing and corresponded with her interesting classmates from all over the world.

 My husband brags to his friends about my new fitness accomplishments, but then brings me junk food and tries every way possible to keep me from going to the gym or for a run. Why?—*Grace*

DEAR GRACE: You've certainly got his juices going. He seems both proud and threatened by the new you. Yes, he's testing your mettle but there's a lot riding on your hanging tough.

Jane hasn't completed her project yet, but her marriage has improved. When she stopped feeding and enabling her husband's addiction with her energy, emotional angst, and drama, he decided to seek treatment and has been sober for two years. Obviously, this was not the purpose of her new pursuit, but there is a dynamic that gets triggered in a relationship when a woman detaches from the problem and redirects her energy to making her own life better.

However, if you are with a man who is very fragile and would be threatened if you were not totally formed around him, your actions could trigger the opposite effect. He may not be challenged by your growth and expand his own horizons but instead may find that someone else would better meet his regressed

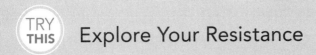

1   Is fear of upsetting your relationship keeping you from
    exploring other ventures?

2   Do you resist reaching out for other experiences because
    you are still stuck on getting most of your happiness from
    your partner?

3   Is it difficult for you to find your own self-support to take the
    risks you would like to take?

needs. This would be sad but ultimately telling, since a strong, beautiful, evolving woman like yourself would probably want to know whether you have to give yourself up to be with him and this would make it crystal clear.

Consider YOUR Mindset You have this one beautiful glorious existence in your fabulous body—a body that even with limitations and imperfections allows you to experience the delights of sensation and the emotions of joy and love. I want that for you. I don't want to see you wallowing in self-pity and delusion, fearful to get what you want to be and do, and hoping and waiting for life to mysteriously get better. If I've convinced you of just one thing, hopefully it is this: you have both the power and responsibility to make your life wonderful. Don't tell me that this isn't possible. I won't let you substitute a weak excuse for a life plan. I won't agree that you are helpless and hopeless. I will insist and demand that you envision what your heart of hearts most dreams of and take one small step today to make it happen. It isn't easy to go against cultural expectations and work through your own conditioning, to confront the resistance when you start to take risks, to begin the trial-and-error process of figuring out what you want and how to get there. You may not be well supported in your efforts and it may take some time and patience, but I know you will do it.

Share YOUR Views *Discuss this chapter in your book club or women's circle, or with friends:*

1 Has it been easy or hard for you to carve out some time for yourself and focus on a dream for your own life? Do you know what your dream is, or will it take some effort to figure out?

2 While you were growing up, how much support and encouragement did you get to develop your talents and skills and focus on preparing for your future? Was it assumed that you would marry and have children, or were you able to see more options for yourself?

3 Are you aware of factors that inhibit women from conceptualizing a fuller life for themselves and keep them focused on the needs of others? Do you think that this is changing?

CHAPTER 12

BE NOW—IT'S WHERE LIFE HAPPENS

Due to our preoccupation with the needs and demands of others, and with the intensity of our multitasking lives, for most women there is precious little time to just *be* and connect with the reality of our existence. There is also an almost universal belief that our best life, our real success or happiness, will occur in the future and this moment is just a dress rehearsal, a time to work for that ultimate payoff. Additionally, many women don't compartmentalize as easily as men and have difficulty finding space for themselves. Ruminating over past hurts and problems and shaping others to meet your needs are time and energy drains; letting go and finding acceptance allows you to be more present.

There are benefits for a woman and her relationship when she can embody herself and find the wisdom that is available for her in that exquisite flesh-and-blood vessel that contains her beautiful spirit. Experiencing ordinary sensations—touch, taste, smell, sound, and sight—can enhance the pleasure of life, especially when it comes to sex and affection. Your intuition and gut instinct are found in your body and help you navigate through important decisions. This vital information would be lost if you existed solely in your mind. Showing up for your life requires conscious effort, but the rewards are great for those of you willing to do so.

Learn to Just Be

Real life is more beautiful than anything you could imagine. Nothing compares with being alive and experiencing the subtle sensations that your body provides. If you make your life into fiction however you will miss out on a tremendous amount of joie de vivre. How do you live in a fictional world of your own creation? By not being fully present in the here and now, the only place where you can feel your own aliveness and experience the fresh raw sights, sounds, flavors, and feelings of this moment.

Stop all the busyness and the mental analysis and just be for a few minutes. It's not necessary to meditate formally, although that can be useful. (There are available instructions on simple ways to meditate—following your breath is the most common.) What I'm talking about here is just stopping and being still. If you are a typical woman, you are among the multitasking geniuses of the world, shopping, talking on the cell phone, and planning a party menu simultaneously, or getting dressed, watching the news, and helping kids with homework. If it's unusual for you to do one thing and concentrate fully on the task, it's even less likely that you'll find the time to sit, empty out your mind, and stop the internal chatter. There is a huge payoff in making the space and time each and every day to be still and silent and to check in with yourself. This is the time when you can sense the larger purpose of your life, the needs and feelings that are deep inside, and take the introspective journey that is, for many women, the most important one.

When you continually fill your days with tasks and to-do lists and strive to get more things done, you believe that is who you are and what you're about. You may see your purpose in life to be orchestrating the household, keeping the kids on task, creating a family life, finding a few friends, and making money—and looking good while doing all of that. If your mind is dizzy with your current responsibilities and problems, and then you do find space, you may find yourself taking an excursion into the past and reminding yourself of things that went wrong or create future scenarios that make you worried. If feelings of emptiness, boredom, or just plain exhaustion take over, you may lose your direction and question your purpose.

Resist Being a Role

Women take their relationships very seriously. You may believe that relationships are your job, that there isn't a separation from your life and the relationships you create. This is why men can better compartmentalize. They have a work section and when they leave work, they can move into their leisure spot or family place. Many women live in one big room without dividers and swirl work, family, relationships, and themselves together in one big crazy stew. It doesn't have to be this way, and if you give yourself a break and sit quietly for a period of time each day you'll begin a process that helps you understand that you are not your roles. You have a self that is beyond what you do, how you look, and how much you accomplish.

Look Inward

Finding space was difficult for Emily with her busy job as a software engineer married to a building contractor who played in a band on the weekends. With a heavy round of entertaining, maintaining her large, beautifully decorated home, and supporting her older teens in their activities, Emily had nonstop days where just eating right and fitting in a little exercise was a challenge. As a child of working class parents she always believed the *good life*, like the one she has now, would be ultimately satisfying and the source of happiness, so she was surprised when she became depressed.

"I should be happy. Life is good. I have everything anyone could possibly want. Why don't you slap me and say, *come back when you have a real problem*," she laughed. I invited Emily to find a peaceful place and look inside herself for answers rather than outside where she had been looking. With her eyes closed, while I played a tape of ocean sounds, Emily tried to respond to my suggestions to imagine herself on the beach feeling the breeze and the warm sun, hearing the birds and the waves, and allow herself to just *be*, but intrusive thoughts got in the way of her focusing. She had many things to do for a dinner party that weekend and was afraid she couldn't relax.

It helps me to get through the day to believe that the future will be better when the kid is toilet trained, the promotion fixes our finances, or I lose the baby fat. What's wrong with that?—*Penny*

DEAR PENNY: Living for the future uses up your time hoping and waiting, and there will always be more to hope and wait for. By focusing on today you won't be missing the pleasures *now*.

Eventually, with patience Emily, could imagine herself at Pfeiffer Beach at Big Sur, her all-time favorite place. *Now, just be here at this beautiful spot and become one with the place, melt into the vastness, the beauty; be that sound. What is it that's important for you to know? How can we frame your question?* I continued my suggestions. Emily was soon able to recognize that she wanted to ask, *what's missing?* The answer she came up with surprised even her.

"*To be*. I need to experience *being* and not so much *doing*. There is always so much to do and it has its moments, but it doesn't really nurture me. I think I do need some alone time,

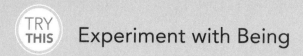

TRY THIS — Experiment with Being

1. Sit quietly at a time and place where you can relax and imagine a beautiful healing spot, perhaps the ocean, a mountain stream, or a wildflower meadow. Just let yourself melt into the beauty and peacefulness this location holds for you.

2. Consider what being can offer you. Feel your aliveness. Sense how your *presence* can be enough. See how activities are repetitive and come and go but your deep connection with yourself is the constant.

3. Make some notes about this experience and what information it held for you.

some down time, some *me* time. I know there's a deeper meaning to my life and I'm just paddling as fast as I can on the surface. I have to stop and see what's important to *me*." Emily said it better than I could.

Being Present Reduces Anxiety

Like Emily, most of the people I treat for anxiety and the depression that anxiety often spawns are living much of their lives fearing a problematic future that rarely materializes the way they imagine. Usually there is a reason that these people evolved into anxious worriers. Having grown up in an abusive household,

Emily lived through a lot of bad times and was always waiting for the next catastrophe to occur. She was continually trying to avoid all kinds of potential problems and imagining horrible events that never happened. Even as an adult in her current reality with a more-than-adequate income, a safe environment, and a good husband, she can't keep herself from fixating on all kinds of catastrophes like financial ruin, health issues, and troubles for her children. By focusing on the simple sensations and small pleasures that are hers today right now she—and you—can move away from the futuristic thoughts that wreck havoc with your mood and drain energy, and feel enlivened in the present.

 Ask Sally I tried to meditate or just be still for a time but my mind just keeps going a zillion miles an hour. What do I do?—*Desiree*

DEAR DESIREE: Your mind will do that for a while because that is what it was trained to do. Keep bringing your focus back to the awareness that isn't moving or changing.

Subtle Messages Are Important

When you spend too much time in your head, talking incessantly, planning, and working, you disconnect from your body, which has a wisdom all its own. It takes a grounded body to understand that something is happening when you experience emotions like sadness, anger, and love, and you need to pay attention. Being cut off from your feelings causes a deadening effect where you experience reactions as thoughts and then roleplay how you think you should feel or behave. Your gut instincts reside in your body and when you can connect with your felt sensations and interpret the meaning they give you, you'll be better able to align yourself with your truth and stay on course for the things that matter.

TRY THIS   Journaling

Journaling can become your way of turning inward and dialoging with yourself about the things that matter. Even if you are busy with a job and family you can find a park at lunchtime, stop for coffee in the midst of running errands, or grab a few minutes at the kitchen table after dinner instead of watching TV. However, one of the drawbacks is privacy. You may be fearful of exposing yourself on paper with the risk that others will read your private thoughts. So, if you can't guarantee privacy, you shouldn't journal, because you won't feel free enough to do it without self-consciousness. There are many ways to do a writing practice:

1   Drain off whatever emotions are on the surface in a kind of rant if necessary. Let yourself have free rein to express how you feel with no regard to spelling or the normal rules of writing. Get everything out no matter how bizarre, irrational, or overblown. Let it be as big as it is.

2   If decisions have to be made, ask your knowingness, intuition, or wise self for direction, advice, or guidance. You can frame it as a question or try this phrase: *take me where I need to go; show me what I need to know.* Clear your thoughts, sit quietly, wait for something to surface, and write it down. Parts of your journal may be a dialogue like a play with your questions and the amazing answers that can come.

3   Use your journal as a time to check in with your life. You may find that the journals become a document highlighting your important decisions and different phases. Go back and reread passages that were important to remember, or look for the signs when a new trend was forming. You might discover that the value far exceeds the time it takes from your day.

If, like my client Shawna, you override your subtle instincts, and talk yourself out of the messages they convey, they become less noticeable and may go away causing you to become clueless about your own map, your inner knowing. Shawna was working long hours, was always attached to her BlackBerry, and worked out obsessively at the gym while plugged into her iPod. For her, being busy was a kind of medicine to numb the feelings she didn't want to look at. She lived for the future when her body would be perfect, her job promotion would happen, and her relationship would be everything she wanted. Instead of focusing on her life now she lived in an imaginary world of her dreams and in the process missed her real life, the good and the bad, the pleasure and the pain. However, more important, she was disconnected from the source of her wisdom, her deep knowing, the basis for understanding herself and making good decisions about her life.

Show Up for Sex

Being present and embodied can be immensely gratifying when having romantic and sexual encounters with your man. Women frequently tell me that they destroy the pleasures of these moments by continuously thinking about such matters as disliking their body parts, tasks they have to do, and planning activities for the next day, all the while wondering why sex is such a chore. If your man is skillful in triggering your body's sensations and bypassing your busy brain, you'll be aware again of how beautiful it is to experience those amazing sensations and delights, but sometimes that is hard work on his part. It would be better if you can notice those thoughts and practice letting them go.

You might even be good at pretending to be sexually involved but all the while staying in your thinking mind. What a loss for you to be a disembodied actress and miss out on so much fun and pleasure. Some women tell me that they can use their brain to get

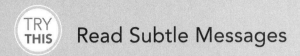

TRY THIS

Read Subtle Messages

1. What gut instincts or intuitive hunches do you get that you ignore or talk yourself out of?

2. How might you distrust your own wisdom and look to others for direction?

3. Where in your day could you find some quiet time to check in with yourself?

4. What issues are you facing right now for which you need some clarity to make the right choice?

themselves in the mood by thinking sexy thoughts, remembering erotic times, and imagining the details that will excite them. This is certainly an improvement over planning the grocery list. However, by practicing moment-to-moment presence with the sensations of seeing, smelling, tasting, touching, and hearing and experiencing embodied awareness like the pleasures of desire and excitement, you can become grounded in your own gorgeous vehicle that carries your life and does so much for you.

Pain May Surface

Suppressed issues may surface when you become still and quiet. It's necessary to resolve these issues in order to feel truly clear and peaceful. You can continue to ignore these things by keeping busy—mentally and physically—but these unresolved issues will continue to present themselves until you work them out.

Instead of interpreting a trauma as a victim, it's critical that you move through the trauma and celebrate your strengthened character as a result of what you endured. Reworking your story and understanding it from the perspective of an adult is an important piece of work, but just as important is mining the experience for the value that it has, the gifts that this particular experience gave you. Sometimes it will require therapy to do this.

Courtney had to learn to do just this. She stuffed all the pain of her childhood and young adulthood into a junk closet and forced the door shut. When she opened it even a crack, everything came falling out in chaotic disarray and she had to work harder to get it under control.

I encouraged Courtney to unravel the story of her mother's long illness and death, the disappearance of her father into depression, grief, and alcohol, and the heavy load of parenting her younger siblings, which fell to her. Some of these images were almost unbearable for her—helping her desperately ill mother as an eight-year-old, feeling scared and powerless watching her dad get drunk. Throughout the telling of her story, I helped Courtney to see that although it was a difficult and overwhelming chapter in her young life, along with the pain and hardship she received something for her efforts that she wouldn't have without these dark times. By recognizing that she learned so much about life, what was important to her, how strong and resilient she was, and that she could find what it took to survive, she knew she wouldn't be the woman she is today without those experiences.

When she released some of her pain she found it possible to be with herself without having to be constantly working. She discovered that being present in the here and now opened her to sensations and feelings that were pleasurable. She enjoyed sex when she could escape from the mind chatter in her head and relax into her body. She was beginning to experience her self without the heavy expectations she had been saddled with from an early age.

Be Here Now

There are numerous rewards for simply being in the present. For one, there is no other reality. This may seem simplistic but it is always now, you are always here, there is nothing else. When you relive the past or think about the future, you are having that experience in the now. A large number of people have a chronic dissatisfaction with their present reality and don't want to be here. They have a continual thought process that tells them that the future will be so much better, that what they are going through now will not be happening later, that life will be as they want next week or next year. So many women are constantly denying or canceling what they have now under the erroneous expectation that things will improve.

The reality is that life will always be a mess, a potpourri of good and bad, at times a painful struggle with a sprinkling of pleasure. There is no perfect place to work toward. Living for the future can be a continual trap—a way to turn our life into fiction. Even when you achieve the things you thought would bring you the good feelings you crave, there is always another thing to attain in the future. It is better to accept and be with your man and the now-ness of your life as they are. This will offer you a greater measure of happiness overall.

Acceptance Frees Energy

It's easy to be open and present when life is good and things are going well. But when you aren't being treated the way you'd like or when you're not getting the attention you expect or want, it can be difficult to accept the present moment and allow it to be as it is. However, by arguing with what is, by resisting things as they are, and by refusing to accept that this is what you are being offered now, you lose your presence. You create negative energy and may stay stuck in that morass for a long time, ruminating and going over the details of what happened, imagining the outcome that would have pleased you and the scenarios that would have evened up the score, and churning up anger and resentment.

 I am a worrywart and think of every possible thing that could go wrong so I can keep it from happening. This is stressful, but how can I stop it?—*Candace*

DEAR CANDACE: As soon as you notice yourself solving an imaginary problem you need to stop and instead convince yourself that if or when a real situation requires your intervention you will be able to handle it. Supporting yourself this way will increase your confidence and reduce your anxiety. It takes practice but the payoff is worth it.

What would happen if you could just accept that this is the reality and let go of judgment, just observe without evaluating? It can become a practice to just allow everything and everyone to be as they are without analyzing, correcting, and deciding what is wrong and what should be changed. The better able you are to let go of these preferences, the more peace and tranquility you'll create for yourself and others. This doesn't mean that the things you can control and change shouldn't be changed. Where you have the responsibility to correct behavior—as in the case of dependent children—then of course that is what you need to do. But where people's words or behavior have hurt you, it's better not to expend the energy to correct them. In these instances, just accept *what is*. I recommend you use your reminder system again whether sticky notes or a bracelet to reinforce this mantra: *let it be as it is.* You will be practicing letting go when you don't have the power or the responsibility to control behavior or events.

Don't Try to Change Others

You may be asking, *if somebody says something that hurts my feelings or makes me mad, you're saying I'm not supposed to tell them about it? How would I get them to change, apologize, or to make things right?* The answer is that you don't. It takes a lot of energy and present time awareness to shape others' behavior to be in line with our preferences and it is rarely successful. Having hurt feelings or anger is a cue that you need to do some work to release them rather than challenge others to change their ways. Your overarching goal is to stay present and keep your heart open and allow things to be as they are without resistance. You create peace within by being unperturbed by life's events as they come. It may not be a good idea to take this path in every area of your life, however. By all means, get what you pay for or correct problems with service or negotiate in the business world. I am only advocating acceptance in the area of relationships and for things that are out of your control. If you work to change or avoid the things that annoy and anger you, you'll always be engaged in this process because there will always be more things to fix in your environment. When you let go you can stay open, present, and positive most of the time. Resisting the present and making it wrong only increases your pain and suffering, whereas releasing it and moving with openness and awareness into the next moment frees you.

My mantra that *you get good at what you practice* is true here. These are ways of being that become automatic as you use them and see how they work. The biggest lesson you'll learn is that you can be fine and centered regardless of how others act. Do not allow their behavior to hurt you, but feel your own power and be centered and grounded in who you truly are.

This way of dealing with life is not to be confused with the indifference or defensiveness that occurs when you must guard yourself from feeling because you're fragile and fearful. Rather, you can remain undisturbed and see that unconscious behavior needs no response. When you continue evolving in this way you can see people who are unconscious as blameless, that if they were capable of a higher level of awareness and behavior they would be there. You can also extend that same grace to yourself when you act unconsciously or remember things you regret from the past.

Consider YOUR Mindset The best thing that *now* offers you is the opportunity to show up for your life. By being present you can find the space apart from doing and thinking, center yourself into your core essence, your deeper self, and be open to the reality of your magnificent existence and all that it contains. It is a right-brain exercise, where you shift from the analysis and judgments of your left brain and thinking mind to a spacious, connected, peaceful place. You also show up for the important people in your life and give them the gift of your presence. Without thinking, without setting your own agenda, without seeing the problems, flaws, and things that need correction, without being reactive or emotionally triggered, you decide to simply be present and take in the words, expressions, and body language of those around you, and experience people as they are. If you think about what it means to smell a rose or feel the soft moist sensation of baby skin, or see the sunset over the ocean, you would awaken to all that you would miss if you live your life in the fiction of your mind.

Share YOUR Views *Discuss this chapter in your book club or women's circle, or with friends:*

1 Have you managed to find a regular quiet time to check in with yourself? What gets in the way of your being present and centered?

2 What do you think of the idea that trying to get people to behave as you'd like consumes energy and is often unproductive? Is it easy or difficult for you to allow things to be the way they are without reacting so much?

3 What strategies help you to slow down and pay attention to the small pleasures, sensory experiences, and joyful moments of everyday life? What interferes with this practice?

CHAPTER 13

THE CURE FOR HOPING AND WAITING

Depression and chronic fatigue affect more women than men, which may happen because women are socialized to focus on others' needs and don't realize that their energy account can become bankrupt. Women who spend more energy than they're making end up in a mental or physical crisis with their chi or life force at a low ebb. Recognizing how you make and spend energy is vital to staying in balance. Soft addictions like web surfing, shopping, and endless phoning, like the more dangerous hard addictions of drugs and alcohol, drain your energy without giving anything in return. Perfectionism, excessive caretaking, and negative beliefs can poison your body and deplete your energy. Sometimes, to enliven yourself and your relationship, you may create drama and blow-ups, devise manipulations, and use emotional blackmail, but the outcome has the opposite effect and you end up spent and exhausted. Identify the ways you may be contributing to your problems and take the steps to reinvigorate your life and your relationship.

Soft Addictions Keep You Stuck

What is going to cure you of the belief that your will always have the time and energy to fulfill your life purpose, that there is no urgency? What will it take to reignite your resolve and recharge your enthusiasm? Do you find yourself hoping and waiting for something to happen that will make your mood brighter, your life better, your happiness greater? Are you waiting for some financial benchmark; for a kid to be potty-trained, graduate from school, or become self-supporting; for a new job to materialize; for a home project to finish up; for you to lose weight; or for the biggest hoping and waiting game of all—your relationship to magically transform? Have you discovered a way to salve your chronic unhappiness or discontent while you're waiting? I call these things that put your life on hold *soft addictions*. These don't destroy your life in the way that *hard addictions*—drugs, alcohol, and gambling—do, but like all addictions they cover up your bad feelings and kill time. Soft addictions include things like talking on your cell phone for hours each day, web surfing, playing video games, watching TV soap operas or sitcoms, shopping, or doing anything that leaves you with an empty feeling and doesn't give you what you want most. However, as with hard addictions, when you stop the habit, the bad feelings—the discontent, the boredom, the realization that you want or need something truly nurturing—are still right there.

 I feel overwhelmed by so many problems—my weight, messy house, unpaid bills. Watching the home shopping channels on TV helps me avoid the stress. How can I stop?—*Jennifer*

DEAR JENNIFER: Make yourself accountable each day for one thing that you must do even for thirty minutes or an hour. You will decrease your stress and chip away at your resistance.

So why don't you step out and do the hard things, take the risks, and make a plan? Most women avoid doing this because it's difficult, requires effort, depends on looking inside, coming up with ideas, taking action, and making mistakes. It's a lot easier to just to go shopping and find a new outfit, or get hooked on a video game where you can find virtual success. Soft addictions keep you from confronting your fear, looking at your belief systems, dealing with your deeper issues. When you lose your zest for life and don't have the will or enthusiasm to do the things you want to do, it's necessary to look at both where your energy is going and why you feel the need to medicate yourself with mindless activities.

Manage Your Energy Account

Energy is not as mysterious as some people think it is. "Why am I so tired all the time?" Violet asks me. "I feel exhausted a lot, not just physically spent but mentally and emotionally spent, too." Each woman has a finite amount of energy—just like money in the bank—and how she spends it determines whether she's getting interest and making more energy or losing interest on a bad investment and depleting her energy. Just as you can go bankrupt by overextending yourself and making unwise financial decisions, you can go bankrupt energetically, which may take the form of depression or physical illness.

Energy is created when you're happy, having fun, enjoying life, and being productive in work or activities that bring us success. All the positive things you do—like gardening, exercising, or having lunch with friends—stimulate your brain to make good chemicals that help you feel positive and upbeat. When you spend a lot of time complaining, arguing, obsessing about things you have no power to change, watching negative news, or feeling like you're going nowhere in life, your brain chemistry reflects that state and plunges you deeper into inertia.

 I'm sick and tired of feeling sick and tired. Chronic low energy keeps me on the couch. What do I do when life is too much effort?—*Lela*

DEAR LELA: You are caught in a downward spiral and breaking out will take changing your thoughts as well as some positive action. You may need a therapist to help you.

Depressed people almost always have low energy, sometimes to the point where they are unable to even get out of bed because their brain chemistry is so out of balance. A few depressed people have a type of clinical depression, a genetic predisposition to a brain imbalance. Most depressed people, however, have a chemical imbalance because they have situational problems and negative belief systems, and have difficulty keeping their energy storehouse filled. They may view their life as hopeless, their personal resources as inadequate, and be stuck in misery. They are losing more energy than they are making and end up in an energy crisis. Sometimes the best way out is to get medical help. Some women live in a constant state of low-grade depression, rarely feel happy, and are unable to find satisfaction or enjoyment in their daily activities, and often just struggle to get through the day.

Physical Effects of Low Energy

Caring for your body requires more than good nutrition, exercise, and medical checkups. There is an energy element that contributes greatly to your mental and physical health. When you're in a chronically depressed and low energy place, scraping by with little vigor or enjoyment, your immune system is likely

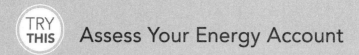
Assess Your Energy Account

1   What is your energy level like? Are you chronically tired, negative, or depressed? Or do you feel reasonable satisfied with your energy?

2   What are you be holding out or hoping and waiting for that you could let go of?

3   What is one thing that you personally could change that would bring up your mood and energy?

4   How can you monitor the negative thinking that gets in the way of feeling good?

to become compromised, and you will be susceptible to illnesses of every kind, from simple colds that linger to virulent diseases. It is no mystery that when you experience a full, engaging, and enjoyable life, all the cells in your body receive the message to thrive and live, and when you're tired and beleaguered the message received is the opposite of this.

You are not divided into a body and a mind—you are one piece and what affects one affects the other. Repeated studies show that our bodies do not separate a thought from what is actually happening; the standard test for this is to imagine biting into a lemon and see if you don't begin salivating. You can poison your body by coloring your existence with negative perceptions or by imagining all kinds of catastrophic things that never happen. As you worry about these terrible events, your body reacts as if those things are actually happening, and generates the hormones and stress chemicals necessary for the *flight or fight* response. These chemicals are not readily dissipated when no action is necessary, which can contribute to a chemical imbalance and an energy drain as you use up your resources on imaginary disasters.

Manage the Needs of Others Selectively

Other people can make demands on your energy and you can find yourself exhausted because you've allowed your friends and family to take up too much of your time and personal resources. When you accept that your energy is limited, it's necessary to decide how much energy you have available to give to others and to set limits and say no to expectations or requests that you are unable or unwilling to fill. It can be difficult to refuse friends and family members who you care about or who have legitimate needs, but there is no ultimate gain if you're overwhelmed and exhausted because you've taken on too much and are suffering under the load.

We can also deplete ourselves caring for others because we believe their love or approval is necessary and we scare ourselves that they will reject us if we don't sacrifice ourselves to please them. One of my clients, having grown up in a family with an alcoholic father, was such a person. She felt enormously responsible for everyone's happiness and was constantly working to do the things that would please them. While her family enjoyed the special handmade gifts and the neighbors were grateful for the lovely casseroles, she was overly dependent on the good will these gestures generated and she feared that without them she wouldn't be as loved or valued. Giving up some of these energy drains, especially the long weekly phone calls to family members,

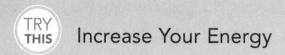

Increase Your Energy

1 Identify the people in your life who are energy contributors, those who make you happy, whom you enjoy, and who leave you feeling uplifted, positive, and satisfied.

2 Identify the people who are energy drains, those who are so needy, dependent, unhappy, and complaining that you end up feeling exhausted when they are around.

3 What are the activities you do that contribute to your good feelings or that give you energy?

4 Consider the activities that are not contributing to your energy and decide if some or all of them can be eliminated.

to focus more on her own needs was hard for her but ultimately she realized her own internal support.

Negative Thoughts Can Be a Downer

We are learning that it isn't necessarily external events like a job loss or an accident, or even other people and their demands that will trigger a drop in mood and energy. Rather it's your own internal voice, incessant mind chatter, or continual stream of thoughts, especially the ones that repeat endlessly. For Allison, her issues with perfectionism contributed to her drop in energy. A good and dutiful daughter of a minister, she was raised by her strict parents to

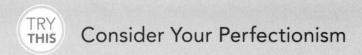

Consider Your Perfectionism

1   In what area of your life would you see yourself as being a perfectionist, having standards that aren't easy to attain or maintain?

2   How could you live with reduced standards in this area, accept that ordinary or average could suffice, and be content with a mixture of success and mistakes?

3   Where are you spending extraordinary amounts of time that is not yielding much pleasure or benefit? How might perfectionism be driving this situation?

4   What would you do with the extra time that might be available if you weren't obsessive about something?

be hardworking, serious, and conforming. Having never received much warmth or praise growing up, she was ultimately hard on herself and was never satisfied with anything. She carried these standards over to her husband Darryl and their three children. "I'm always looking at what's wrong in everybody. I amuse myself in meetings or waiting in airports to just look at people and see what's wrong with them. I can't seem to turn it off. I do it with the kids and especially with Darryl. I want to tell him he's eating too fast, his shirt is the wrong color for the tie, or that he's gaining weight. I've probably complained of at least twenty things he does that bug me." Allison recognized her own perfectionism in the fact that she seemed obsessed with her children and saw her job as a mother reflected in their behavior and performance. While she celebrates their successes she is often preoccupied with little problems and worries about how they are developing. I helped Allison see that all this obsessing, judging, and complaining affected her energy and mood. She acknowledged that she learned this behavior from her critical mother and that it comes from a caring place, but the criticism doesn't feel good to her—especially when she's been particularly mean.

Perfectionism is one of those qualities that can affect women profoundly and rob them of good energy. It may be hard to recognize since usually it does not affect every part of your life. There will be only one or just a few areas that receive your intense focus.

"I can't be a perfectionist; my house is a mess and I rarely do anything with my makeup. Why would you think I'm a perfectionist?" Violet thought that perfectionism was a total thing. However, when she looked at her work and her fitness schedule she could see that there was almost an addictive quality to them. Nothing was good enough in those areas. She always wanted more from herself. Even when she got an award at work she didn't feel it was deserved and, despite her grueling gym schedule, she thought she could do better, use heavier weights, and so on. Violet was holding out on herself, believing that she would feel good about herself when she measured up to her ideal. In reality, she was hoping and waiting and instead of gaining energy from these activities, which consumed a lot of her time. They became a downer, a drain, and a constant reminder of what wasn't good enough in her life.

Another client used her weight as a way of not feeling good about herself. She was constantly negative about how she looked and the size of her clothes, and let the scale tell her whether it was going to be a good day or a bad one. Not surprisingly her soft addiction was food, and when she was feeling especially low-energy she stopped for a cinnamon roll or decadent coffee drink. She also focused her perfectionism on creating a perfect home with professionally decorated rooms like a showplace. Her hobby became endless shopping for the most unique accessories to complete the special look. This used up energy that could have benefited her in more personally satisfying ways.

Drama and Blow-Ups Drain Energy

Most women recognize how a big blow up consumes their energy, makes them feel angry and hurt for days, and provides some measure of excitement in the making-up process. This kind of drama is a huge consumer of energy and keeps you going nowhere. Some of my clients, when they don't have the motivation to get the real pleasure they want from life, substitute drama as a synthetic way of feeling alive. They create drama in their relationships to relieve boredom, project irritation and negativity, or just provide some necessary change for feeling stuck. Often being critical and complaining can start a blow up. Sometimes just acting out where you say very little but show how hurt, upset, or distressed you are can elicit the attention you crave. Of course, drama is a big downer that you want to avoid. If you are using drama as a way to spice up your life, it's important to take a look at how you're creating it.

 I get so little attention from my husband that getting him to fight with me is better than his normal indifference. What do I do instead?—*Caroline*

DEAR CAROLINE: Spending your life force to generate negative energy is not a good exchange. Stop wanting what you can't have and go after something, anything, that nets you even a small satisfaction. It's a start.

Consider Drama

1 How do you spark some drama, create some tension, or stir up your relationship when your life situation isn't what you want?

2 What do you get for the expenditure of energy?

3 What might you create with the energy instead?

Polly owned up to causing drama in one of our sessions. "I'm a drama queen! I admit it! If I can't get attention from Sal in a positive way I will go in the bedroom, act upset, and refuse to answer him when he invariably asks what's wrong. I know what I'm doing but I can't help it." I explained to Polly that drama is a manipulation—a way to engineer someone's response by saying or doing something that isn't honest or accurate. Many women learn this trick early in life. They want to subtly control someone. In Polly's case she is seeking attention so that she doesn't have to deal with her own loneliness, boredom, or emptiness.

I explained to her that those feelings of loneliness, boredom, and emptiness are important to experience. They are what fuel your desire and motivation, and they help you find out what you need to do to make your life what you want it to be. However, it's easier to create drama and make your feelings be about your man instead of doing the work necessary to focus on yourself.

Take a First Step

1 What would you like to do, have, or be that doesn't require someone or something else to change?

2 What do you do most days that zaps your energy and time and gives back very little in the way of real joy? How many hours does it consume?

3 What is one small thing you could try today, right now, that would feel positive?

Get Unstuck

You may feel defeated or stuck and not know where to begin to reinvent your life. As a young social worker, I worked with abused women who were ambivalent about leaving their violent husbands. Most people made the mistake of advising them to leave and expressed incredulity that they couldn't make a decision that looked like a no-brainer. These women were depressed, depleted in energy, feeling worthless, and so unconfident in their ability to make changes in their lives that the task of leaving was absolutely daunting. My supervisor at the time, a petite sage of a woman said something I've always remembered: *Get them to change one thing they want to change—their hair color, their kitchen curtains, anything! Soon a whole ripple effect will be started as they grow in strength and self-support. Next comes a class, getting a job, or learning to be assertive. It's a process!* I think this is true for everyone. You need to start with one small thing that is doable. Don't condemn yourself and decide that if you can't transform your life in a day that you'll have to stay stuck.

 This is your prescription. Start by taking a big dose of courage. Accept that you can be a force for good in your life, relationship, family, and the world and realize that overflowing with energy is the only way that your life purpose will manifest itself. Don't wait another minute! Begin today to be present and do what is necessary to keep your energy storehouse full. Eliminate one soft addiction that kills time and zaps energy. Change one negative belief system that drops your mood and makes you tired. Check yourself when perfectionism and judgment try to take over. End the drama that hurts your relationship with your man. Find one new thing that regenerates your energy and enlivens you. These are little steps with big payoffs. I love your goodness, your caring, and your desire to be a powerful presence in your life; I know you will make it happen.

 Discuss this chapter in your book club or women's circle, or with friends:

1 How are you able to regenerate energy and stay balanced? Who or what can you count on to keep you feeling positive?

2 What are the energy drains you need to plug? What people or activities give little return for the expenditure of energy? Which situations have to be tolerated for now?

3 Which soft addictions consume your time and energy? What thoughts or beliefs sabotage your energy and good feelings? What would you be doing with the energy if you were able to curtail or stop these wasteful practices?

CHAPTER 14

GET THROUGH THE HARD STUFF

Growing into a stronger, more resilient person involves recognizing the ways you use your partner and friends. Acting out was necessary when you were young and required your caregivers to find resolution for your problems. Then you could only express your moods and feelings with drama and gestures. Now, as an adult, you must express your emotions responsibly and negotiate for what you need. A mature woman has found the internal resources to tap when the going gets rough and does not need or expect constant soothing and support from her man. When your man's aid and comfort *are* needed, understanding his nature and preparing him for what is requested will ensure a better outcome for you. Otherwise, he may not be able to decipher what is needed and go into his normal pattern of either acting defensively or trying to fix the situation. Remember, it would be unusual for him to seek this kind of assistance. In this chapter, I offer methods to help you strengthen your own self-soothing abilities and weather the normal ups and downs of life and relationships on your own. These are useful tools that will help you cope with distress and tolerate the pain of negative emotions when it is not desirable to seek comfort elsewhere.

Help Your Guy Be More Responsive

You may expect that your man will be your go to person when you're experiencing intense emotions, but he's likely to be more available and supportive if the situation triggering the pain is not related to him or his perceived failures. There are times when a woman, in her desire to be heard and understood by her partner, will escalate the drama in an effort to convince him of her pain and heartache. It is natural for your man to be defensive and unavailable when the problem causing you so much misery is said to be his fault.

Barbara became unglued when she discovered Tony had added some expensive hunting equipment to their already overextended credit card in preparation for an equally expensive trip with two buddies. When he wouldn't listen to her or look at the bottom line on their checking account she began pushing him and striking him in the chest, screaming, and crying. He held her wrists and yelled back causing their two girls, seven and eleven, to leave their TV program and join the fray. Later that evening after she dropped the kids off for a birthday sleepover Barbara went to the mall and bought four hundred dollars in clothes to match his expenditures. After not sleeping or eating, feeling angry, and unable to attend to her normal chores, Barbara was a wreck when she showed up for her appointment.

"Of course you would be angry. I certainly understand how you would see his behavior as irresponsible. Finding it out the way you did is doubly disturbing." I empathized with her plight. Barbara thought that to convince Tony that what he did wasn't okay she had to pull out all the stops. However, in reality, Barbara was the one hurt when she spun out of control and got so upset. I helped her see that she needed to find ways to manage her intense anger, and understand that it is fueled by her need to control Tony and that it doesn't actually change his behavior.

She now recognizes her anger as it starts to escalate and reminds herself that it isn't going to help the situation.

He May Be More Available If He's Not the Problem

When the problem causing pain is something or someone other than your partner, he may be able to support and help to soothe you. But it's good to define specifically, if you can, what it is you want from him, rather than expecting him to figure out on his own what you need and provide it. You could say something like this: *I'm so upset about my friend Dawn getting diagnosed with cancer. I just need to talk with you about it and maybe have you hold me.* If the problem is something ongoing you can say, *I know you've heard so much about this, and you may be tired of it, but I need you to listen to the latest problem she's having.*

 I'm a revengeful person and always try to get even or hurt people who hurt me. It doesn't make me feel better though. What can I do about it?—*Denise*

> DEAR DENISE: You already know that expending your energy this way doesn't do the job. Try resolving the pain by allowing people to be as they are—unconscious, uncaring, or indifferent.

If you proceed to be upset and cry without first helping your man prepare himself, you may not get the support that he would be able to give you if you did. Your man may misinterpret your mood as a complaint about him, launch into defense mode, and not be able to hear what you are saying. He may not be able to figure out on his own what you need from him in these circumstances since he is unlikely to freely express his fears, anxieties, sadness, and other vulnerable feelings and does not reach out

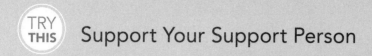

TRY THIS Support Your Support Person

1 Is your man as supportive and interested in your feelings and problems as you want him to be? How could you help him understand better what you need from him?

2 How have you used tears, anger, or emotions to solve a problem with your man and found that it backfired or only escalated the issue?

3 Would using other support persons or falling back on your inner resources be more appropriate than depending on your relationship for most of your emotional needs?

for support and comfort as easily as you do. This is probably unfamiliar territory for him. Men have difficulty being receptive, listening, and comforting without offering concrete suggestions. It is their nature to solve problems and fix things. It is not an indication of love and caring so please don't make this into a test. Instead give him a heads up and ensure the best outcome for yourself and him.

Barbara took my advice and was amazed at the success she had on her first attempt to involve Tony in their budget problems. "One night I invited him to have a glass of wine with me after the girls went to bed and go over our bills together to make some decisions about how to handle the payments. I told him honestly that I needed him to help me sort things out, that I felt overwhelmed. She reported that there was no arguing or blaming, that they discussed things calmly and he made some notes about how they were going to manage the credit cards. "We went to bed and cuddled. It actually made us closer."

Understand When It's Too Much

If you need your partner for comfort, support, and soothing on a regular basis and are using him daily as a sounding board about every kind of stress—your job, your mother, the kids, the frustrations of everyday life—you may be doing what is called dumping, asking him to be available for a daily avalanche of anger, disappointment, and problems. It is an error to think that this is the purpose of your relationship, and your man will eventually become worn down by listening to this emotional outpouring.

 I want my boyfriend to know and understand me, which is why I tell him everything about my life now and what I went through in the past. Is this a good thing?—*Rose*

DEAR ROSE: It may not be possible for him to really know you, and the volume of material that he must absorb may be burdening your time together. Consider writing a memoir instead.

You may not be sensitive to your man's response when you begin your daily monologue as he turns off, tunes out, and wonders how he can get away without stressing you further. This is the true mark of a high-maintenance woman, someone who not only needs constant attention, love, and reassurance, but who is also emotionally dependent on others and has few or no inner resources. If you don't want to exploit the energy of those you care most about, you would do well to develop your own internal assets. This is not easy, but the payoff will be hugely rewarding as you discover that you can be autonomous and less affected by the normal things that will continually happen in life.

Learn Where You Need to Grow

As a therapist I look at a person's behavior—especially how they handle emotions—for clues to their level of maturity. Just because a person has reached chronological adulthood does not mean that their emotional maturity is on a par. On the emotional spectrum, the infant is of course the most immature. A baby cannot identify what she needs and can only cry to get attention and help. Contrast this image with a fully mature woman who takes complete responsibility for what she needs. She develops reciprocal relationships, provides for herself, and has a wide range of things that satisfy her—groups, churches, work, sports, volunteerism, pets, and so on. In sharp contrast to the baby, she is not dependent on one person to know and supply what she needs. She weathers difficulties, stresses, and loneliness with substantial inner resources as well. All along this continuum there are varying degrees of health. As you mature and use the lessons that life provides to you, you'll advance in your capability to support and care for yourself.

Recognize Immaturity

When a person cannot directly express her anger or negative emotions in a responsible way, the usual indirect option is to act out. The woman engaging in this behavior usually wants to roleplay her emotions, punish the offending person, or get revenge for having been wronged. However, expecting someone to figure out your behavior and correct the situation should have ended with middle school. Using words to communicate problems and resolve issues is the mark of an adult.

Giving someone the cold silent treatment or withdrawing affection and communication is a common way that women try to get back at their partners. This type of behavior is commonly

Evaluate Your Maturity

1 How well are you able to be responsible for yourself and what you need? Do you have unmet expectations from others?

2 How often do you fall into the role of a victim and believe that your difficulties in life are because of your partner or globally because of bad luck?

3 Are you able to see the bigger picture of life, its shades of grey rather than black and white?

called passive aggression, which is when you submerge your feelings of disappointment or anger and get even in subtle ways that you can later deny or pretend were accidental.

For example, when Tony took a trip to see his elderly mother in a nursing home and failed to call Barbara for several days, she began screening her calls so she could deliberately not answer when he did call. In her mind, this would create some tension or concern for him as payback for his inattentiveness to her. When she finally talked to him she denied the manipulation and claimed she was busy and even apologized for not being available. If your man pesters you about your weight, you can say you're too tired to go out with him rather than expressing the hurt directly. If he works late many nights but then expects you to be instantly available when he takes a rare night off, you can make up a pressing conflict with a girlfriend to get even. You get the idea. In situations of passive aggression, the perpetrator can hurt herself as well as her partner but the need for revenge seems satisfied. The tit-for-tat passive aggression in rela-tionships can cause escalating damage as an act of revenge by one partner can trigger a corresponding action by the other.

It's useful to know how to respond if you are on the receiving end of a passive-aggressive partner. You ask him to do something and he forgets or does it slowly or poorly. After a disagreement, he gives you the silent treatment, but when you call him on it he says he's just tired. He says he'll meet you at the therapist, but doesn't show up and claims he was held up at work. Confrontation never works in these situations because the objective of your man's behavior is to avoid what he doesn't want to do or punish or anger you and get away with it. Your best approach is to be empathic, to rise above your irritation or disappointment, and accept his excuse. Say something like, *I'm sorry it didn't work out for you, yes, it is tiring to have such intense discussions,* or *I wish you didn't have to miss the session but I understand those things happen.* By not getting angry or upset you thwart the intended purpose of the ruse.

Depersonalize Hurts

Many women need to look for the cause of their upset inside themselves rather than instantly assuming that another person caused the pain. For example, a person with continual hurts may place the blame on someone else rather than seeing that they reached adulthood with numerous sensitivities and unmet needs leftover from their childhood. Are you still bothered now if you were not given enough attention as a child? If you were not val-ued or appreciated or were criticized, is that what you are sensi-tive to with your partner? Just allow yourself to feel the way you feel and don't put the blame on your partner. It is natural and normal to have unfinished business from our childhood and this is a good way to resolve it. When you are able to tolerate the bad

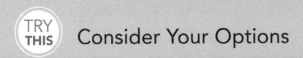

TRY THIS

Consider Your Options

1 Identify the ways each of you may be acting out emotions or using passive aggression where a direct approach would be better.

2 What is at risk if you use a direct approach to express what you want?

3 In what areas of your relationship would acceptance be preferable to confrontation?

feelings from the past and recognize where they came from, they will work themselves out without you having to try to change the behavior of your partner, family, and friends. When you can allow these feelings and just be with them each time they arise, they will lessen in intensity. When you resist experiencing them, are scared by them, or depend on someone else to take care of them for you, you strengthen the power they have. You may not realize that feelings will pass through and change on their own and that, while they feel bad at the time, if you can stay centered and tolerate them you will grow in maturity and resilience.

Try Self-Soothing

When you take responsibility for your emotions and manage them maturely, you'll begin to realize that there are many ways to do this. It will be a developmental process for you to explore various coping skills and techniques as you allow your intense reactions and feelings to work themselves out and discover that you can create your own peace and serenity. Here is a sample of tools that I have shared with clients over the years. Some may already be familiar to you.

Writing

Whether you keep a regular journal or not, when your mind is full of dialog and rampant chatter and you fixate on the same issue and keep running it over in your mind, a writing exercise can be a way to make a clear space in your head. Free to express yourself, it's possible to destroy your writing afterward so you don't have to worry about others reading it. If you like, you can write a letter—but not mail it—to someone to whom you need to give a piece of your mind. Or you can address your writing to your higher or wiser self, and ask questions in a meditative way that may yield answers or advice. You could also engage in a cognitive type of writing where you look at the pros and cons of a situation, evaluate the options, think about what else you could do, or consider how you could think differently about what's going on. You could also take the opposite position from the one you hold and challenge your thinking.

Distraction

It is possible to give yourself a reprieve or mini-vacation from intense upset feelings by coaching yourself to do something that you need to do or usually would enjoy doing. This may be something like baking a batch of muffins or cookies, cleaning out a drawer or closet, mopping up the kitchen floor, or paying the bills. You could watch a TV program, read a book, or try on outfits that need updating or coordinating. You might go somewhere—to a movie, the mall, or the gym. You may need to coax yourself to do these things as a way to take your mind off of a problem that doesn't seem solvable in the moment.

Physical Comfort

When you need someone to hold you and no one is available or willing to do that, it may be necessary to devise your own comforting regimen. You will need to think about the things you can do based on your own unique preferences. Would you like to wear something silky or soft, an old familiar garment that feels just right, or just wrap yourself in something fleecy or wooly? A warm bath or a hot shower—especially one with fragrances or lotions that appeal to your senses—can help wash away a bad mood or a clingy emotional layer. Stroking and petting yourself or using a massage tool on your shoulders can be satisfying as can be rocking in a chair.

Exercise

Simple exercises like stretching, a few minutes of yoga, or a walk of just a couple of blocks can help to change your mood. Intense exercise is a powerful tool that can reduce anxiety and dispel depression. Whether you run, work out at the gym, or swim laps there is the greatest likelihood that you will find profound relaxation afterward with an increase in both your energy and mental focus.

Music

Music is a powerful mood-changer and listening to music is a wonderful way to soothe or re-energize yourself. Finding dance music that makes you want to move either up-tempo or with a smooth flow can move your emotions as well so that the stuck places change. Just listening to music and finding the artists, albums, or songs that speak to you can help you cry or express what wants to come out. You probably have your favorite pieces that will touch you in the ways that you need.

I always thought that depending on each other for emotional support helped partners to feel closer and make a relationship stronger. Am I mistaken?—*Joanne*

DEAR JOANNE: If the sharing is reciprocated by your man, then it may have a bonding effect. In many cases, however, it's a one-way street with him doing the heavy lifting.

Sensory Comfort

Your senses can be stimulated in ways that calm you. Scented candles, incense, and essential oils can help you connect with your internal self and offer respite from excessive thinking and obsessing. Flavorful teas or cold, tart beverages like lemon-spiked club soda, or hot chocolate have their appeal, as do cinnamon toast or savory foods like salty cheeses or nuts. Petting animals is another traditional comfort that has been proven to offer health benefits such as reducing one's blood pressure. Looking at a plant, pictures of a landscape, or photos of a wonderful trip, your children, or grandchildren can be satisfying too.

Arts and Crafts

Artistic expression is not just for the talented among us who can create beautiful sculptures or paintings, but is a way for everyone to suspend judgment and criticism and just *be* for a spell, allowing what isn't available in words to surface through art.

You can use simple materials like markers or crayons or more sophisticated materials like paint and canvas. Crafts like beading, quilting, knitting, and reclaiming recycled materials take concentration and allow you the opportunity to connect with another aspect of yourself, which can also be gratifying.

Nature

Our animal essence craves nature. This may not be easily accommodated by city living. Spending time by a pond or lake, walking in a park or on a trail, and watching birds—perhaps the only wild species readily available—or studying flowers and trees, is necessary to refresh and renew yourself and to shed the heavy emotional issues that may burden your mood. It may be that remembering your place in the natural world helps you realize that you are more than the problem or issue that troubles you.

Find Your Own Wisdom

You may be like Elizabeth who resisted my suggestions that she learn to soothe herself. Her pattern was to depend on her husband Carter or call her mother on the phone. She called her mother four or five times a day seeking help or advice or just wanting to chat. Carter was upset and thought Elizabeth was sharing too many of the intimate details of their life with her mother, which made him uncomfortable when they visited her parents. Elizabeth was startled when I suggested that she may be a married woman with twins but in some ways she hadn't actually left home or her mother but had one foot in each place. "I love my mother. We're best friends. Are you saying I shouldn't be calling her?"

I explained that it isn't how often she called but how she used her mother that gave me that impression. Elizabeth may be shortchanging her own growth by relying on her mother's wisdom instead of her own. I also saw how she was triangulating her relationship with Carter by confiding in her mother so much.

Elizabeth was curious about the word triangulate. I asked her to look at the three of them—Carter, her mother, and herself and decide where is the strongest bond. It isn't between Carter and her mother. "Is it between you and Carter or you and your mother?" Elizabeth understood the point I was making and worked out a plan where she would manage problems she was having in her marriage on her own or with Carter. I suggested that she give her mother a heads up on this to let her know that she was trying something new. It's likely that Elizabeth's mother may feel left out and try to stay connected with her daughter in the old way and it will take some additional strength on Elizabeth's part to keep her marriage separate. Elizabeth was also going to learn how to manage her own emotions better rather than immediately unloading on her mother and depending on her for comfort and soothing like she did as a girl living at home.

Consider YOUR Mindset Again, you can see how your relationship can motivate you to look at your own issues and grow in maturity. Seeing yourself as a victim without choices only empowers the perpetrator you imagine is keeping you in this position. By recognizing your own power and resources you don't need to blame others for your problems or become defensive and reactive. When you are firmly grounded in your own truth, you won't need to defend your position. There is rarely a benefit to blaming, complaining, and confronting. Instead, accepting the situation and letting action flow from that place will result in a better relationship. Understand that learning to manage your own emotions will open the door to using the coping skills available.

Discuss this chapter in your book club or women's circle, or with friends:

1 Do you agree that women naturally want to share their experiences and feelings as a way of getting close to their men? What strategies have you tried to help your partner be more available?

2 What immature behaviors do you still hang onto that no longer serve you well? What happens when you try to use them?

3 Since childhood you have probably been learning ways to soothe yourself. Which of the ideas presented are ones you are familiar with? Which new ones do you intend to try?

CLOSING THOUGHTS

I hope that you are able to look again at your good-enough man and realize that it isn't necessary or even desirable that he be a prince or that you find a happily ever after. There is so much value in accepting both him and yourself the way you are and growing in strength and wisdom as you confront the reality of your life together. As a woman, just as you've been conditioned to accept an unattainable model of beauty, so have you been sold an unattainable relationship model. A relationship is just one part of your life and you need to see a bigger picture in order to satisfy yourself and reduce the expectations that a man will be your ultimate fulfillment.

By moving away from suffocating and confining cultural definitions that have trapped you in relationship conflict, you can find your truth, authentic self, and natural power base. By accepting both your own and others' imperfections and knowing that your worth is not affected by what others say and do, you can stay open, loving, and compassionate. As an empowered woman, you can stand in your truth and ask for what you want without demanding to receive it. You can reduce the need to contort and deny yourself in order to be loved. There is enormous benefit for a woman who can conceptualize her task as evolving herself rather than fixing her man.

I have thoroughly enjoyed writing this book and sharing my own life lessons and those of my clients with you. This book is filled with what I wish someone would have told me when I was a younger woman. It is imminently satisfying and blesses my life to offer it to you.

Index

ABOUT THE AUTHOR

Sally B. Watkins, MSW has been a psychotherapist in private practice treating individuals and couples for the last twenty years. She holds a bachelor's degree in education from Carnegie Mellon University and a master's of social work from the University of Maryland at Baltimore. The mother of two grown sons, she lives with her husband in Northern California. She welcomes your comments or feedback at *www.sallywatkins.net.*